To my frie...
calks. The best f...
your future.
The Magnemions,

Leading Out Loud

Leading Out Loud

The Authentic Speaker, the Credible Leader

TERRY PEARCE

Jossey-Bass Publishers • San Francisco

Jossey-Bass books and products are available through most bookstores. To contact Jossey-Bass directly, call (888) 378-2537, fax to (800) 605-2665, or visit our website at www.josseybass.com.

Substantial discounts on bulk quantities of Jossey-Bass books are available to corporations, professional associations, and other organizations. For details and discount information, contact the special sales department at Jossey-Bass.

For sales outside the United States, please contact your local Simon & Schuster International office.

 Manufactured in the United States of America on Lyons Falls Turin Book. This paper is acid-free and 100 percent totally chlorine-free.

Library of Congress Cataloging-in-Publication Data

Pearce, Terry, date.
    Leading out loud : the authentic speaker, the credible leader / Terry Pearce.
        p. cm. – (The Jossey-Bass management series)
    Includes bibliographical references and index.
    ISBN 0-7879-0111-3
    1. Leadership.   2. Communication in management. 3. Public speaking. I. Title. II. Series.
HD57.7.P4 1995
658.4'092–dc20   95-14574

FIRST EDITION
HB Printing 10 9 8 7 6 5 4

CONTENTS

PREFACE

▼ Leaders, by definition, move other people to change. But in the past decade, cynicism and fear have increased substantially among the public, and enthusiasm to embrace any leader's call for reform—be it in business or government—has been considerably dampened. In the face of this negative shift in attitude, many leaders attempt to motivate by threatening livelihood or offering.rewards. Compliance, however, is no longer adequate to gain competitive advantage or to solve social problems. Increasingly, leaders must instill commitment in others rather than merely demanding compliance. People must take individual and collective responsibility for the accomplishments and failures of their organizations or governments if those organizations are to thrive.

The unmistakable conclusion of contemporary social research is that people are eager to commit. They are truly starved to connect with competent, trustworthy leaders. The rapid pace and enormous scale of change have stripped away all vestiges of security, leaving the public in dire need of stability—stability not offered by leaders or officials who change principles with the latest poll or quarterly report.

Ironically, as the public hungers for connection, technology and "spin doctors" push leaders further away from their audience. Concurrent with the growth of cynicism, expanded media influence and the growing authority of professional image makers have combined to exacerbate the problem, to distance leaders from the people who can make them successful.

Speaking is a vital part of leadership, and though we know intuitively that the power of speaking comes from authentic conviction, we increasingly evaluate speeches by their cosmetic appeal rather than their effectiveness at moving listeners to committed action. Most speakers are content with the superficial criteria because they seem easier to master. Doing a technically good speech seems more concrete and simpler than being authentic and powerful. Listeners are content with surface criteria because they are reluctant truly to engage with a leader who is advocating change. It is much easier to find fault or to praise technique than it is to entertain the possibility of personally acting to alter a familiar existence and move into a new future. And finally, communication professionals find it difficult to coach or direct a speaker in a way that will bring conviction to the forefront, enabling expression from both the head and the heart. Such coaching is, by its nature, more demanding; it requires a deeper level of involvement than merely writing better language or making observations about physical habits.

Audience

Leading Out Loud is written as a tool for speakers and communication professionals to bridge the gap between symbolic and substantive speaking. Anyone who is interested in being effective as an advocate of change can use this book. It is a guide to real self-expression, and its use can transform a speech—what to some is an uncomfortable experience—into a moving encounter for both the speaker and the audience. The concepts and practices form an excellent template for any communication. Accordingly, it will be helpful to anyone who wishes to influence others. The work is the culmination of nearly three decades of experience as an executive and coach. In every part of my career, I have found wide responsiveness to these ideas. In fact, I have found a great need for a guide that would encourage and assist people in tapping their own source of conviction.

Overview of the Contents

The book is organized into four parts, each with two or three chapters. Part One reviews the link between leadership and speaking, tracing the changing requirements of leadership, reinforcing the importance of communication, and making the case for authenticity as a requisite for effective advocacy. The second chapter of this part provides ways to discover and articulate basic values that fuel your own personal convictions.

The remaining parts—corresponding to the beginning,

middle, and end of a speech—are written both to recommend the type of material to use in a powerful speech and to suggest ways of relating that material to maximize the possibility of commitment from the audience. Part Two discusses the opening portion of a speech, looking at conventions and showing how conscious attention can establish credibility and begin to build trust. Part Three addresses the middle of a talk, pointing out the importance of context and suggesting the organization and content that will engage both the minds and hearts of the audience. The examples illustrate the most effective use of supportive data, and encourage you to employ personal experience, analogy, and metaphor to inspire authenticity and lift the speech beyond the mere delivery of information. Part Four considers the end of the speech, reviewing the elements of an effective conclusion and the importance of an individual call to action. The second chapter in this part deals exclusively with the question-and-answer format and suggests a method of considering questions that requires a speaker to remain authentic, conscious of both the stated and unstated agendas of a questioner.

Because I believe that the requirements of leadership speaking are changing, I have based my analyses on contemporary examples. Although some of the speakers quoted may not be familiar to you, all are quite successful in their fields, and I felt that it was important to provide representative samples from business as well as the public sector.

The requirements of leadership in the modern world are daunting. As people move toward a recognition of interconnectedness and as information becomes a widely available commodity, the realization of the relative nature of all things will continue to affect our world. Leaders simply must reconnect with what is unchanging, what will confirm a basis of common reality. Authenticity can reopen the door to common ground and a sense of stability. *Leading Out Loud* has been written to contribute to that possibility.

Acknowledgments

Because this book presents a departure from traditional views, it was a long time in the making, and the ideas were subjected to several tests of credibility. When the concepts were little more than topics of conversation, Jim Nunan gave me an opportunity to develop them into a method to teach corporate executives how to speak more effectively. For his courage, I owe him a great debt of gratitude.

I'm similarly indebted to Richard Snyder, who three years later offered me a chance to teach at the University of California, Berkeley. His faith in this approach allowed the expansion of the work into a course at the Haas School of Business. Since then, I have been supported by an ardent group of students, some of whom are mentioned in the writing, and most particularly by my teaching partner and friend, Ralph Tolson, and by Dean Andy Shogan, who champions the cause of communication as a legitimate professional skill.

I suspect that writing any first book requires substantial spiritual support for the idea as well as for the author. I have been blessed with both. Brother David Steindl-Rast provided spiritual inspiration throughout, and Gary Fiedel, Steve Hamilton, Luisa Adams, Kathy Thulin, Peter Sussman, Leni Miller, and Jim and Vicki McNeill were constant sources of strength, providing ongoing positive messages and suggestions. An advisory group read early versions of the manuscript and offered ideas that improved the work immensely. This circle included Clint Cheveallier, Ned Dean, Larry Hammons, Yves Huin, Pat Larkin, Jim Losi, Alice Mayn, Andy Mecca, Jeff Rosenthal, Emily Scott, Gene Stone, and professional colleagues Carol Fall, Mark Davis, Geri Blitzman, and William Miller.

I drew heavily on the magnificent work of Harvey Stone for some of the concepts in Part Two of the book, and Tom Steding's lecture on the history of business consulting influenced the material in Chapter One. I thank them both for inspiration.

The editors at Jossey-Bass, Sarah Polster and Barbara Hill, displayed patience beyond reason and provided pinpoint criticism and suggestions. Their expertise and insight demanded an entirely new level of consideration from me. The book is richer by far as a result, as am I. Sarah's remarkable attention to purpose also gave birth to the title of the book.

Paula Nichols brought the manuscript into form with hours of tedious attention to detail. She also displayed her own considerable writing skill with laserlike editorial comments.

Three people took nearly full responsibility for the completion of the work. Steve Walch was a superb coach, providing expert advice at the most critical times. Gerry Oliva would not let my own enthusiasm wane. She provided the kind of gentle pressure and listening that can only come from a deep and abiding friend. David Pottruck, president and CEO of Charles Schwab & Co., was confidant, contributor, and practitioner par excellence. He is just simply the finest leader and the best speaker that I know.

Finally, and with all my heart, I thank my children. My daughter, Jodi, has taught me the measureless value of authenticity as we have struggled to connect. My sons, Jeff and Joel, have often cooked meals, put up with long hours, and missed fishing trips in order to accommodate the demands of the work. Their faith throughout the months of this process was just extraordinary. Without them, there would be no reason for the work. Because of them, the work felt absolutely imperative.

Novato, California   Terry Pearce
May 1995

THE AUTHOR

▼ **Terry Pearce** is founder and president of Leadership Communication in San Rafael, California, a company that consults with corporate and political leaders on communicating to instill commitment to change. Terry is grounded in business, having spent seventeen years as a manager and executive with IBM before starting his own firm. Since 1989, he has taught speaking and leadership development at the Haas School of Business at the University of California, Berkeley, where his courses have received the highest ratings from graduate students for being useful, effective, and relevant to their futures as leaders in the business community.

Pearce's clients include top executives of Fortune 500 companies as well as senior public officials and elected leaders. His program is featured in the catalog of The Executive Briefings of the Stanford University Alumni Association, and he is a frequent speaker on the subjects of leadership and communication.

His interest in the relationship between leadership and

speaking was kindled during his college years in Oregon. He earned his B.S. degree (1965) in business from Linfield College, where he also became increasingly interested in religious philosophy. His concentration on inspiring action was further focused during the mid 1980s when he frequently traveled to the former Soviet Union working to pioneer U.S. business activities. He is cofounder of Partners, an international company that continues to market consumer products and facilitate joint industrial projects in Russia.

Active in his community, Pearce served on the board of and participated in the American Trans-Continental Relay, staged to endow a national drug and alcohol resource center. He currently serves as director of the Healthy Communities Project of the Institute for the Study of Social Change at the University of California, Berkeley, and as managing director of the Partnership for a Drug-Free California.

Pearce has three children and lives in Novato, California.

PART ONE

MAKING CHANGE HAPPEN

Speech as a Leadership Tool

▼ This book is written for leaders who believe that public speaking is vital to their success. I propose in these pages that the way in which we have judged speaking in the past fifty years is no longer effective; indeed, the old public speaking tenets are counterproductive to the ability to lead successfully in the age of information. This is not because the old methods were wrong but rather because what is required to inspire people today is far different from what it has been.

The end of the modern era has brought with it a well-documented confusion of values and a substantial shake-up in fundamental beliefs. Much of the world's accumulation of information is universally available, and as a result, the people with the most knowledge no longer have the same leverage to gain leadership positions. In fact, the seemingly unlimited availability of information offers more confusion, more possibilities, and the average person is left groping for certainty. And in groping, we are searching for what is real, what is authentic, what will form the new foundations of the postmodern era. Many of us feel a deep disconnection between the world we live in and the world depicted by Madison Avenue and the media. Life is not what it is advertised to be. We no longer experience our day-to-day existence as simplistic. Answers to pervasive problems are not available in the short term. Accordingly, as leaders speak to us, we are no longer listening for some information or images to believe; we are probing, consciously or unconsciously, for someone to trust. Before leaders can speak to this growing need in an audience, they must be aware of the reasons for the disenchantment and then perhaps rediscover the sources of their own passion to make things change. This first part will address these two aspects of powerful speaking.

1

LEADING IN THE AGE OF INFORMATION

The Growing Hunger for Authenticity

▼ Great leaders have always emerged from experiencing things as they are in the real world, in the world inhabited and experienced by the people who are most affected. Franklin Delano Roosevelt identified with the common man and woman. John F. Kennedy and his brother Robert, despite their wealth and aristocratic upbringing, touched the hearts of ordinary Americans. Kennedy's speech in Berlin was a benchmark in identifying with a population that he barely knew but seemed to understand.

In industry as well, the people who are followed with commitment are those who are not afraid to experience and articulate reality. They are followed not because they have all the right answers but because they are perceived to have experienced the same confusion and contradictions as the rest of the population. They address questions that are relevant to the workforce, questions that others also grapple with daily. Authenticity is obvious when such leaders speak. Of course, some leaders equate authenticity with "softness," and feel that to be real is antithetical to producing results. Nothing could be further from the truth, and for evidence, one only need look at the results achieved by leaders we most admire.

Unfortunately, communication coaches, speechwriters, and leaders themselves employ tools designed to cover up reality with cosmetics. No rules for speaking can guarantee that a speech will generate meaning and trust. Current customs only ensure the sparkling appearance of the speaker and the avoidance of offending language. They do not contribute to a sense of authenticity.

Authenticity is hard to develop and even harder to coach. Because authenticity is a *way of being* as a speaker rather than *something you do* as a speaker, few instructions are helpful. Consultants advise, "Just be yourself," which is instantly interpreted as "Act as you would like yourself to act." Of course, doing that bears little resemblance to being oneself.

The responsibility for authenticity, then, reverts to you, the speaker. Through a combination of introspection and discipline, you have to find your authentic voice and amplify it so that it resonates with your listeners. Such introspection and discipline applied to a public address can even become a regimen for leadership as a whole. A coach can only advise you where to look and then recognize and call your attention to your success.

Here is a simple example. In the spring of 1994, the CEO of a major brokerage firm was planning to speak to two hundred of its managers about changes that were occurring in the organization. Like many companies, this firm had recently made substantial alterations in the structure of the company and in the way they did business. The executive was to speak about two significant events: the move of nearly five hundred people from the West Coast to the mountain states and the institution of Saturday hours, which involved keeping the branch offices open for four hours on the weekend to serve customers better. He had prepared his speech to spell out all of the details of both moves. He would outline the rationale behind the changes, look at the increased business that the firm expected, comment on the efficiencies that would result, and finally describe the future of this growing firm and explain what such growth could mean to everyone in the room.

An excellent speaker, he had done a beautiful job of composing the outline of the evidence. His listeners were going to get all of the facts that they needed to be convinced of the business viability of the changes. The CEO had planned to open his talk this way: "I am excited about speaking with you tonight regarding the changes we have planned. Saturday hours and the new concentration in the mountain states will make us even more responsive to our customers. As we grow into the next decade, we will be seeing similar changes for the same reason—to serve our customers better while we provide more leverage for our own growth."

We had been working together for more than a year, and he called me two weeks before the event to consult on his remarks. When we considered the likely impact of the speech on the audience, we concluded that all of the managers would happily comply with the changes. But this executive wanted the full commitment of this management team. He wanted his people to execute the changes with the enthusiasm and dedication of a family.

So as always, we focused on what the speech could do to line up his managers behind the moves, to let them know that they were valued and to gain their commit-

ment to follow his lead. He ultimately began his remarks
like this:

> When I decided to speak to all of you about these
> changes, I was quite excited. As you know, we have been
> considering both relocation to the mountain states and
> opening the branches for a few hours on Saturday for
> some time.
>
> But as I reflected on the impact of these changes, it
> occurred to me that the relocation did not require *me* to
> move from *my* home, and in fact, *I* was not going to
> work any more hours on Saturday than I already do. My
> kids are used to my irregular hours, yet I still value my
> time with their sports teams and the other weekend time
> we have together. For many of you, an occasional
> Saturday away from the family will be something new,
> and certainly, these changes will cause some disruption
> in the family patterns of your staffs.
>
> It also occurred to me that I wasn't going to be
> telling my staff about moving or working Saturdays.
> Rather, I get to address the big issues, while *you* will be
> conveying the news to individuals and dealing with their
> very specific questions.
>
> Given these thoughts, I quickly realized that you
> might not be as excited about these moves as I am, even
> though these changes are for the good of the company
> and ultimately will create more opportunity for all of us.
>
> So this evening, I want to outline the rationale for
> the changes, let you know what tremendous effort has
> gone into the business planning, and speak for just a
> moment about the impact these changes will ultimately
> have on our company's growth rate. Then I also want to
> spend some time discussing the considerations we all
> went through about the personal impact on you and

your families. Many of you have been involved in this
planning.

 After that, I'd like to deal with as many questions as
you have and listen to any further ideas you might have
to make it easier for all of us to realize the benefits with a
minimum of disruption.

These changes did nothing to alter the logical content of
the talk or the eventual action of the managers, yet the new
version set an entirely different tone for the speech and required something entirely new from the executive. He was
not only going to engage his *mind* for the talk, but he was
also going to reflect on the *meaning* of the subject to himself and to his audience. He would engage both his mind and
his heart, and consequently, he would engage both the mind
and heart of each manager as well. By looking not just at
the practical but also at the real human impact of the changes
on both himself and his audience, he was able to relate his
own experience and to connect *authentically* with the group
of managers. We made similar changes throughout the speech,
retaining the logic and strength of the explanations but adding
elements that required deeper reflection and specificity from
the executive and would evoke that same response from the
audience.

 The day following the speech, he invited me to listen to
the voice mail from some people who had heard him. The
remarks did not merely compliment the speech; they com-
plimented the man. Whereas the original speech allowed him
to *direct a corporation,* the final product allowed him to *lead
the people* in a company, a distinction that is at the heart of
our changing business and political environment.

 It is relatively easy to determine and explain what needs
to be done to enhance corporate or community performance,

but it is challenging indeed to inspire others to follow with enthusiastic action. People will do as they are told to meet the requirements of their jobs and to protect their families, but they will no longer be loyal to a leader who merely provides better information than someone else.

Undoubtedly, some executives and other leaders who read this already feel overtaxed by the demands of their publics. Many of you leave it to a professional staff to draft your remarks. Some of you are concerned with the legal ramifications of every word you say—and with good reason. Our society has made it difficult to make even the most honest mistakes. But the corporate and political worlds are spending millions to determine what inspires the real participation of people. What I will suggest is an investment in reflection, direct participation, and practice that will pay great dividends.

The Changing Voice of Leadership

For the past twenty-seven years, I have been involved in leadership and speaking, first as a corporate executive, then as a citizen diplomat, and finally as a consultant and teacher in the field. I have seen a continual erosion in the effectiveness of leaders such that the subject of leadership itself is now among the most studied in business and political academic circles.

In 1994, there were more than two thousand books in print on the subject. Over the previous three years, the United States Congress authorized $10 million to develop "new generations of leaders in the areas of national and international affairs" and called for papers from academic institutions to accomplish that purpose. The best leadership consultants are commanding more than $20,000 per day from corporations, and there are few complaints about value. Yet the basic requirements of leadership have been defined consistently from John Gardner in the 1960s to Warren Bennis in the 1990s: leaders see what is needed and inspire others to take action to effect change.

Just as this fundamental definition has been constant, the entire world in which we operate has been erratic, and we have moved to the edge of a social and psychological chasm. We are confronting this abyss personally, as is each of our potential followers. The change that is now required for success is no longer merely incremental; it is discontinuous, radical, and frightening. We are not simply being asked to "do better" than our predecessors; we are being asked to "do different." As a leader, you are faced with inspiring followers to take this same kind of risk, to jump this chasm with you.

What do followers fear?

The End of Stability

No promise of permanence is believable. We have seen physical and intellectual boundaries disappear with ever-increasing speed. Chaos theory in science, the "reinvention" of business and political organizations, unexpected changes in the map of the world, redefinition of the family, changes in the relative roles of men and women—all of these suggest fluid movement that defies understanding or rationalization. Indeed, the forty-year conditions of the cold war provided boundaries that allowed countless world political figures the luxury of a predefined field on which to lead. That boundary no longer exists, and these leaders will continue to feel the real challenge of their time in office—in effect, to redefine the geopolitical context for the next century.

Business leaders are feeling the same pressure. In the past ten years, American companies have had to turn their organizations into more responsive businesses, changing the very core of employment stability in a company. What was secure work in the old world is now frequently defined out of existence. Employment stability is fundamentally gone. When I left International Business Machines in the early 1980s, I had seen the rhetorical dilution of what had been called a full-employment policy until the mid 1970s. As fiscal reality set in, the policy became the full-employment "practice" and then the full-employment "tradition" before it dissolved into layoffs in the early 1990s.

In November 1994, the director of the University of Michigan's consumer survey summarized the anxiety and insecurity that grip much of the population: "For the first time in fifty years, we are recording a decline in people's expectations, and their uncertainty and anxiety grow the farther you ask them to look into the future."[1] Job, career, and company no longer offer security. Anyone who wants to lead must offer stability of a new kind, a stability that does not come from these traditional forms.

Talent, Not Title

Even more basic than a job, a university education or highly developed job skills have provided a foundation for economic security. Before this decade, during periods of change, people could use their education and skills to improve their lives, to earn a new title with expanded responsibilities. Now the ongoing revolution in technology, rapid changes in geopolitical reality, and redefinition of business functions have rendered degrees and previously developed skills nearly irrelevant. More frequently, it is the talent to master new skills that determines success.

People feel as though they are each adrift in a boat of their own on an ocean of transformative change. They have their old skills on board but no rudder of ordained authority with which to steer to their own destiny. People feel that they have absolutely no control. As Margaret Wheatley puts it in *Leadership and the New Science,* "These stairs of understanding we are climbing feel different. They are less secure, harder to see, and much more challenging. They require very different things from us. . . . We cannot expect answers."[2] What *can* we expect? Wheatley suggests that all we can expect is new information. Yet more information, which we will continue to get in greater quantity than our ability to process it, only means more possibilities; it does not mean more certainty. More information adds to the confusion.

Leaders cannot simply be more knowledgeable than others and thereby be more effective. The old rules for incremental change are not useful for jumping chasms because to do so in two jumps is considered bad form, and people must be more than *mentally* convinced to move forward.

Individual Commitment Rather than Compliance

At the same time that our walls are crumbling from events seemingly controlled by others, we are being held responsible for building the new walls ourselves. Leaders are correctly telling their audiences that they must be individually accountable for the economic and social results of the organization.

I had the privilege of speaking to a session of an *Inc.* magazine conference in 1990 in Orlando, Florida, and found myself following the keynote speaker for the day, Peter Ueberroth. Of course, this could have been either good news or bad news, depending on what Ueberroth planned to say. He could have completely preempted me, or worse, he could have contradicted what I had in mind. I had fashioned my own talk around the idea of instilling commitment in workers by designing jobs with the same attractions as the work they did as volunteers. There was only a slight chance that Ueberroth would say something that would provide a launchpad for my own remarks.

As it turned out, he spoke in very broad terms about the requirements to be successful in the next decade. His remarks neither reinforced nor contradicted my prepared text. I stayed for a moment to thank him and then asked him what question he was most frequently asked. Reflecting on his experience as chairman for the Los Angeles Olympic Games in 1984, he offered, "People want to know how we made a quarter of a billion dollars on the Olympic Games." Naturally, I asked him the secret, and he said, "I tell them that if you organize seventy-five thousand people who are committed enough to work as volunteers for no pay, you'll make two hundred and fifty million dollars every time!" I had a great opening for my remarks.

In all of human enterprise, in every community and business, we are growing more aware of our individual responsibility. This awakening is causing us to look for the solution to social ills from within the community rather than from government bureaucrats and to ask for business solutions from individual workers rather than waiting for instructions from the CEO. We are counting on individuals volunteering to do their part to rid streets of drug dealers. We are looking to citizens to be responsible for their health habits that may lead to serious illness. We are trying to tap the knowledge and skill of individual workers to be more effective.

Margaret Wheatley uses a metaphor from quantum physics to illustrate the advantage of wide participation:

> In the traditional model, we leave the interpretation of information to senior or expert people. . . . [These] few people, charged with interpreting the data, are, in fact, observing only very few of the potentialities contained within that data. . . . [But if] the wave of information spreads out broadly everywhere in the organization . . . many moments of meeting—hundreds, even thousands of them will occur. . . . Instead of losing so many of the potentialities . . . [we will see] many of these potentials . . . [and be able to] discuss, combine, and build on them. . . .
>
> It would seem that the more participants we engage in this participative universe, the more we can access its potentials and the wiser we can become.[3]

I like this metaphor because it casts the problem and solution as the release of energy from *engagement* rather than *instruction,* which is indeed accurate. The new leader must personally engage and must somehow inspire others to do the same.

Personal public speaking is the gateway to this new leadership.

Trust and the Speaking Profession

As public anxiety builds, the communication of leaders has reached a zenith of flimflam. Rather than modify our measurements of the effectiveness of communication, we have strengthened our old criteria by using new technology and asking the same questions that were useful in the 1950s. More than ever, the professions that surround public speaking emphasize entertainment and cosmetics rather than substance. More than ever, we strive to make clients look good, avoid mistakes, and deliver flawlessly.

Our willingness to accept these old criteria is driven by our failure to maintain focus on the purpose of speaking: to move others to action. Professional coaches often make one of two fundamental errors. First, even the best guides to speaking use examples exclusively from people in leadership positions. The question of their real effectiveness as leaders outside of the authority of their position is not questioned. Unfortunately, this mistake is also made by many people who sit in positions of authority. As I interview potential new clients, many feel that learning to speak more powerfully is wasted effort. "After all, I may be a bad speaker, but I am still the boss. They have to listen to me anyway."

Audiences do not have to listen. Certain audiences may have to keep their backsides in the seat while "the boss" talks, but real listening is not required. More important, audiences can never be required to act with any more conviction than it takes to "go through the motions." As we shall see, *required* action differs in both quantity and substance from *inspired* action.

The second common error is confusing the *source* of greatness with a *description* of greatness. Professionals resolve to study the *exterior of a speech* when the real power of it is in the *interior of the speaker.* Attending only to the exterior of a speech brings with it a series of "tips" and "rules," which might provide cosmetic improvement but will not in themselves provide any lasting impact on an audience or, more important, on the leader either.

This second fallacy is easily demonstrable. I often ask students and clients to identify the most effective leaders that they know and then look at the source of their power as speakers. Invariably, names such as John F. Kennedy, Martin Luther King Jr., Barbara Jordan, Winston Churchill, Mario Cuomo, Ronald Reagan, and Adolph Hitler are mentioned. (Business executives rarely make the list, but for lack of exposure rather than ability.) Few students can tell me about JFK's gestures, which were often jerky and awkward. Few people believe that Barbara Jordan's ability to inspire is contained in her posture, yet even confined to a wheelchair, she is able to arouse people of all races and political philosophies.

Certainly, these leaders had a command of their language, but as students point out, what stimulated others was neither the rhetoric nor the show; it was the conviction of the speaker, the passion for his or her cause, the extent to which that passion and that conviction were conveyed, and whether the speech connected with the real experience of the audience.

Few of today's leaders speak their own minds, much less their own hearts. Most, in fact, feel that they have to speak to their followers like ventriloquists' dummies. They follow scripts fashioned, to a great extent, by media and communications specialists and by their own carefully cultivated need to be politically or legally correct.

Media professionals run campaigns for office, and public relations firms control the "voice" of a candidate or chief executive. Attorneys, speech writers, "spin doctors," and coaches suggest and orchestrate what is said between CEOs and workers, between officials and voters. In large part, the leaders play a tune that is written by others.

A recent *New York Times* article, frightening in its candor, characterizes what happens in the United States capital as a charade with a language all its own in which the president and many of his aides are scripted and moved like marionettes through a series of communication shows, ranging in complexity from a simple "leak" to the press to the very complicated and staged "town hall meeting." In such a system, the largest gaffes are described as "naked moments," when the true person actually appears to the public. "A single such event," the article avers, "can permanently scar a public figure." We are told by good authority that "wrong lies in the gaucherie of displaying passionately held convictions. (Stage passion is fine, but it is crucial to know the difference)."[4] The public's perception of perfection has driven what is said by political leaders.

A more significant influence drives the need to sound politically correct in business, where misstatements by leaders can and do end up as evidence in court and where victims, some real and some merely opportunistic, use these statements to show discrimination or other wrong. This is a substantial risk.

Media and Technology

Television and computers have contributed to the central irony. While our overuse of media, voice mail, and electronic communication has increased our need for authenticity, the requirements for "professionalism" in the use of media have minimized the possibility for real expression among the people who use it to communicate. As much as we may want to be in touch with the *real* person, the one we see on television or hear on radio has already been scrubbed clean with the steel wool of a script, makeup, rehearsal, voice lessons, and all the other fixes that can be applied to simulate perfection. Dialects, errors, and other human foibles that are so much a part of the authentic self are absent.

Even in a "live" performance, technological aids mask the leader. The *London Times* recently described the use of the TelePrompTer, a system of transparent screens positioned to the side and in front of the speaker to show the script of what the speaker is to say. The device has been used for years in politics and is now spreading to the world of business speaking. The author, Matthew Parris, ends the article on point:

> We [the public] unconsciously recognize media-speak, and discount it, keeping the information it conveys at arm's length. We have a special compartment for talking heads.
>
> In Brighton last week, John Prescott, in a speech which was almost gibberish, lit a fire in the hearts of his audience which seemed unmerited by anything he said. He did so because he was answering a great, unconscious public hunger for direct communication from our . . . leaders.[5]

That hunger will simply grow. We all know that floating somewhere in the atmosphere of virtual reality, television fantasy, and print media that urge us on to perfection, there is the deep meaning of the real world, the one with warts, mistakes, grief, and passion. In our lack of stability, we are recognizing the value of the firm ground of the authentic. It is the only ground we will truly trust.

The Case for Authenticity

In this context, personal public speaking is again being recognized as a vital leadership skill. Charles Handy, former executive and current lecturer, futurist, and professor at the London Business School, writes clearly about the need for authenticity in the coming age. "Integrity," says Handy, "comes naturally if you live for your vision. In other words, the vision cannot be something thought up in the drawing office. To be real, it has to come from the deepest parts of you, from an inner system of belief. The total pragmatist cannot be a transforming leader."[6] Like most thinkers in the field of leadership development, Handy recognizes that being aware of one's own convictions, being true to them in advocacy, and acting consistently with those convictions are *all* required to gather committed followers.

One of the few leaders on the world stage who recognizes this need for integration and brings the reality to his public life is Vaclav Havel, president of the Czech Republic. He commented on this growing requirement for the authentic in his address to the World Economic Forum in 1992: "Sooner or later, [we] will be faced with the task of finding a new, postmodern face. A [leader] must become a person again, someone who trusts not only a scientific representation and analysis of the world, but also the world itself. He must believe not only in sociological statistics, but also in real people. He must trust not only an objective interpretation of reality, but also his own soul; not only an adopted ideology, but also his own thoughts; not only the summary report he receives each morning, but also his own feelings."[7] Havel has followed these convictions with a withdrawal from doing substantial business with the People's Republic of China, taking a stand in action that is consistent with his inner conviction and his rhetoric.

Toward Introspection in Business

Business needs are also driving us toward authenticity. The commercial community cycles through new productivity theories and practice with regularity, to the point where cynics refer to the next new idea as the "flavor of the month." Although any individual theory seems to be disjointed from others, when seen as a forty-year continuum, these theories reveal a consistent movement from external to internal focus.

In the 1950s, improved productivity was seen as a result of making the human being more efficient. Time and motion studies, carried out by efficiency experts, dealt with workers as one would deal with parts in a machine. The experts looked at the business externally, as though it needed to be more finely tuned by a mechanic. In the 1960s and into the 1970s, business became engrossed with strategic thinking. Peter Drucker and later Michael Porter became the chief proponents of such long-range and market-driven planning. Again, this theory required looking at the business and its resources from the outside, but it focused on "core competences," reflective of the particular skills of workers and the competitive advantages inherent in those skills.

Late in the 1970s and into the 1980s, the Japanese began to dominate many world markets. "Corporate culture" improvements were seen as a way of emulating the Japanese style of management. This broad consideration of human relationships within the organization was a substantial departure from earlier theories in that for the first time, internal process became the focus. "Total quality management" required commitment from workers. "Self-directed work teams," "bubble" organizations, and more open lines of communication were the forms for implementation of such cultural improvement. These forms are clearly aimed at gaining more commitment from individual workers in order to enhance the results of the entire company.

Good management practice has moved from a purely external analysis of the business as an entity to a focus on the internal motivation of the individuals in the company. With this movement has come a greater requirement for leadership that recognizes and values deeper human needs and for leaders who are closer to workers, more communicative, and more vulnerable.

Where will the trend take us? The talent that business now needs to compete in the world economy can come only from greater fulfillment of employees at work. The "learning organization" requires leaders who are actively engaged in the process, who continue to set the pace and direction from the front but are also in the middle, encouraging themselves and others to learn and change more rapidly.

The daunting government challenges of rising expectations and shrinking resources can be addressed only by a committed citizenry. Political leaders who will be effective in this environment must recognize and articulate reality as the constituents experience it and call them to engagement. There must be greater congruence of our values at home, at work, and in our communities, and this will require leaders who can speak to us, understanding and participating in this integration.

A few years ago, Tom Melohn, at the time the chief executive of North American Tool and Die, started a minor but growing revolution in business communication by actually engaging his employees in "town meetings," communicating with them personally and frequently. Melohn and his team went on to build NATD into a company that became a premier supplier to Silicon Valley, then sold it to its employees. Melohn's formula for leadership had only six steps, the first of which was "Be yourself."[8] Melohn has given hundreds of lectures, been featured on a PBS series, and written a best-selling book, *The New Partnership,* and his commitment to being authentic remains at the heart of his message.

Town meetings are now common in most organizations, both business and political. Leaders are frequently required to speak to large groups in a way that ignites the audiences' desire and willingness to take responsibility for their organization and to act. A leader must be able to address issues, answer questions, and "touch" informed audiences. Our measurement of effective speaking must deepen to encourage long-term substantive impact.

Natural Language, Natural Movement, Natural Fire

Authenticity calls us to respond. A graduation speaker at a small college in the Northwest recently told a story that illustrates the difference between authentic speech and informative speech. Actor Charles Laughton was attending a Christmas party with a large family in London. Well into the evening, the host decided that the guests should each read or recite a favorite passage that reminded them most of the spirit of Christmas.

Laughton's turn came near the end, and he recited, in his beautifully trained voice, the Twenty-third Psalm. Everyone applauded his effort, and the process continued. Within a few minutes, everyone had participated except one adored elderly aunt, who had dozed off in a corner of the room. The family gently woke her, explained what was going on, and asked her to take part. She thought for a moment and then began in her shaky voice, "The Lord is my Shepherd, I shall not want. . . ." The room hushed as she continued, and when she finished, tears were dripping down every face.

Upon leaving, one of the younger members of the family thanked Laughton for coming and remarked on the difference in the response of the family to the two recitations—in one case, appreciation; in the other, deep connection and involvement. "How do you account for it?" asked the young man, shaking his head. Laughton looked at him and remarked simply, "I know the psalm; she knows the Shepherd."

The beloved aunt had not planned her performance; it came from a place far removed from any plot to impress an audience. She found, on her own, the proper experience that allowed her to remain in her real skin for the occasion; indeed, she never for a moment slipped out of it.

Speaking from the Inside Out

Can leaders likewise touch deeper values in themselves as well as in their audiences? Can they communicate practical solutions with greater substance and meaning? In other words, is it possible to speak authentically, from both the head and the heart? It is. As a leader, you can inspire commitment by looking inward first, by becoming aware of what you want to say and by communicating a much more personal vision of the future, based on a much more personal knowledge of the past and realistic experience in the present. Such a focus means initially ignoring your audience in favor of your passion.

If you want to escape the fear of imperfection, it makes far more sense to focus on losing your self-consciousness than on pleasing your audience with proper movements, eye contact, and appearance. Speakers who develop their text on the basis of what others want inevitably end up playing to their listeners and trying to please them. But judging your own performance against a standard that is in your mind takes all of your concentration. There is no room for monitoring what you really want to say. And your listeners' reaction will be different. At the crowd-pleasing speech, they may be entertained, but at the other, they will be excited and will grasp new and real possibilities from your own authentic experience.

Speaking as a Discipline

Ultimately, it is your ability to tap into your own human spirit that will inspire others to act, and that takes discipline. Contrary to the popular view, speaking authentically does not mean "winging it." In fact, left to say whatever comes to mind, most of us will try to be entertaining, will attempt to make others comfortable, and will have little influence on change. Yet as we have seen, a carefully enacted rehearsed message can also leave an audience devoid of a connection to reality.

Authentic is not synonymous with casual or formal, rehearsed or spontaneous. It arises out of a discipline of self-discovery and self-expression and seems to be a lifetime process, even for spiritual teachers who practice authenticity as a life's work and who spend much of their lives in solitude. Because many of us feel so threatened by public speaking, we are willing to pay strict attention to it. Accordingly, it is an excellent discipline to practice engaged leadership, to force ourselves to find our authentic power and connect with others.

Of course, not every speech is a chance to advocate a new order of things. You will often speak merely because someone asks you to. Some speeches are commanded by the nature of your position. Sometimes you will choose to entertain, to preside over a ceremony, or just fill a hole in the speaking schedule.

But leadership is fundamentally about inspiring change. The balance of this book defines a process to find authenticity and apply it in public speaking. Though you may apply the principles in every speech, you will find these ideas particularly useful when you wish to change others' commitments and inspire them to move in new directions, despite their misgivings. To move others, you must first know the source of your own strongest convictions. The process of authentic speaking begins here, by discovering what you are compelled to change.

2

CONNECTING WITH YOUR AUDIENCE

The Disciplines of Authentic Speech

▼ Speaking is the bridge between vision and action. Accordingly, the first step toward *authentic* speech is to identify and clarify your personal foundation values, the themes that underlie and support the changes you wish to lead. Through a process of reflection, writing, and careful structuring—that is, including the components and material that compose a complete and compelling communication—you can hone your axiomatic convictions into speeches that let others know who you are and what you stand for.

Discovering What Matters

Determining your own vision of what is needed and what change is required calls for personal reflection, not merely reading good management books. An authentic vision of change doesn't just appear out of the ether, nor does it progress from what others believe to be important. *Your* vision of what you want to change grows from the foundation of values that have been formed by your life experience. These values are vital to you personally, not because they are socially acceptable, although they might be—not because they look good on a plaque on the wall—but because you have *experienced* them to be true.

Warren Bennis, who has studied leadership perhaps longer than any other American scholar, continues to stress the necessity of such self-knowledge. When reflecting on his own performance as president of the University of Cincinnati, he found that when he was most effective, it was "because I knew what I wanted." It was that experience that drew Bennis to define the first competence of leadership as the "management of attention."[1] He continued to stress this need for focus on the delineation of individual values: "Anyone who wants to express himself fully and truly must have a point of view. Leadership without perspective and point of view isn't leadership—and of course it must be your own perspective, your own point of view. You cannot borrow a point of view any more than you can borrow someone else's eyes. It must be authentic, and if it is, it will be original, because you are an original."[2]

I'm dismayed by the number of men and women who have retired from leadership positions decrying their failure to take time for personal reflection while they were active in their post. Rather than initially considering the impact they might make on the organization and then proceeding from a foundation of values, they defined themselves as they went along, at first accepting the old tenets of the organization and only gradually discovering what was important to them personally. This trial-and-error method of leadership results in an inconsistent message and a lack of commitment by the people engaged in the enterprise.

Leaders who make a transition from an old set of dominant values to one that reflects their own beliefs make a substantial mark on the organization. Those who do not make that transition become caretakers and are often replaced when the enterprise faces its first significant challenge. John Sculley successfully made this transition at Apple; John Akers at IBM did not. Ronald Reagan successfully made the transition as president of the United States; George Bush did not.

Successful leaders speak frequently and effectively about their convictions. Former New York governor Mario Cuomo, arguably the best speaker in the United States today, reflects on his motivation to speak in his self-edited compendium *More than Words:* "For me, the vital thing is that there is something important I want to say. . . . As I look back over the speeches I selected for this volume, I note that most of the things I was trying to say revolved around the small cluster of basic ideas that have resonated with me for most of my adult life."[3]

These core ideas (the rule of law, insistence on a sense of responsibility, the rejection of the melting pot for the mosaic view of our multiculturalism, the need for seeing our disparate society as a family, the belief that work is better than welfare, and the idea that "economic growth" is the provider of the American dream) are the topics for Cuomo's best preplanned speeches, the ones he considers his most definitive. These speeches define Cuomo as a leader.

You, too, will find that there are a small number of ideas that constitute the core of your philosophy. Delineating your point of view is the first step toward speaking authentically.

Two Approaches: Questions and Stories

I've used two methods to encourage reflection on values. Whereas individual beliefs can be discovered by asking specific hypothetical questions, reviewing an entire life story can reveal much more of a person's overall system of values and the relative importance of those values. In my class in leadership speaking at the Haas School of Business in Berkeley, each student works with a single speech for the entire term. I ask students to choose a topic by answering one of three questions:

1. What single value is so important that you would teach it to your children as the most important foundation of a happy life?
2. What condition in your chosen industry would you change and how?
3. What is the most important social issue we have to deal with as a community (world, nation, state) and how would you correct it?

Students are required to have had some personal experience with the issue that will illustrate how they formed their position on the subject.

Speaking about these topics reveals some real conviction in the students. In addition, they realize before term's end that the topic questions are interlaced; that is, their values create their conviction, whether it is about the value itself or about one of the applications of the value in business or society. For example, one of my students recently chose to speak about the preservation of the environment, imploring his audience of M.B.A. candidates to take steps toward conservation of natural resources. This is a fairly common topic in California, as many people are environmentally conscious, especially on university campuses. Accordingly, it is difficult to move an audience to further action; people believe that they are already doing enough.

But Rob Nicholson was different. A native of Canada, he related his own personal experience of observing lakes near his hometown lose their fish population to acid rain. He quoted a space shuttle astronaut's observation that there were only two manmade landmarks visible from space: the Great Wall of China and a massive old-growth clear-cut in his home province. He was highly credible, as he had studied environmental science as an undergraduate, but he also made an authentic connection with his audience through his strong personal conviction, an outgrowth of his personal experience.

Rob could draw on this environmental experience to speak metaphorically to business or political issues. The preservation of capital, the efficient use of by-products, the idea of personal responsibility for the greater good—these topics and others could be addressed using these same events to stimulate his own conviction. The strength of this speech resulted from Rob's reflection on a single question and his use of the answer to construct the content of the speech.

As you can imagine, contemplating an entire life story will often reveal a whole array of individual values and shed light on their relative importance. Accordingly, I ask each corporate and political client to write or dictate an autobiography as a first step toward learning to speak authentically.

I request that clients pay particular attention to events in their past that seem like turning points, events that have prompted fundamental decisions about the relative importance of ideas, things, and behaviors. We then use these events to construct speeches around fundamental themes, drawing out the individuals' authentic concerns.

In late 1994, I worked with the executives of a small company in the San Francisco Bay Area to help them redefine their vision and values. In my interview with the founder and CEO, I discovered that he had been orphaned as a boy, started his business as a very young man, and delivered his product to customers from his own secondhand truck. In addition, he had been divorced twice and had tragically lost a teenage son in an accident. He of course has many specific vivid memories of these events.

The company has grown to three hundred employees and nearly $150 million in sales, but it still exemplifies the basic values of the founder. Is it any wonder that he emphasizes a strong family feeling, independence, and the need to serve the customer above all else? To this entrepreneur, these values did not come from a quick read of popular management books; they came from his life, and they carried with them all of the authenticity of his own passion and conviction.

Every idea that you hold passionately has a background in your personal experience. Two of the bases of predictive psychology are that our beliefs are a product of our past teachings and that things learned through actual experience and personal observations have more power to form our future than ideas learned by abstract examination.

The Greeks claimed that our life force is guided by a *dai-*

mon, an attending spirit who defines our destiny. Our daimon, the Greeks believed, invites us to certain life experiences and keeps us from others to further our development.
James Hillman, today's most noted archetypal psychologist,
compares this daimon to similar beliefs in other traditions:
"Hindus speak of karma; Romans would have called this
ghost your genius. . . . In our century, [the angel] has reap-
peared as Jung's 'Wise Old Man' and 'Wise Old Woman,'
who, he says, are configurations of the guiding Self."[4]

By contrast, much of today's psychology regards many of
our most influential and most powerful past experiences as
occurrences to live down or recover from. Certainly there are
cases where recovery is needed; but our feelings, compassion,
and conviction and our dedication to study are strengthened
by our entire past, both "good" and "bad" experiences. At
the extreme, the most compassionate and effective counselors
are those who have themselves experienced tragedy, addic-
tion, or poverty; and the strongest leaders are those who have
experienced or personally witnessed the negative effects of the
status quo and the subsequent transformative power of change.

As the world turns more and more to technology, the pri-
macy of our humanity will assert itself. Real life is still primary to technology. We will never discover our passion and
conviction from a computer. Only reflection and human interaction will aid us in discovering why we are here and what
we are to do.

Each of us has something unique to say, and it is based
on our particular makeup and our rich and sometimes dire
experience. To speak as an authentic leader, you have to listen for your own daimon and find the themes that are

most important to you. You can then convert them to inspiration for others.

Writing Speeches: Disciplining Your Voice

The insights of reflection require the discipline of writing to be converted into action. Although off-the-cuff remarks can *seem* authentic, they often relay only the emotional impulse of the speaker. We have all heard speakers who can "light a fire" in an audience. When such a speaker is finished, everyone in the room wants to do *something,* but no one knows what to do. Conviction that moves others to action includes both passion and reason. Authenticity is vulnerability joined with competence. Both are necessary to generate trust and action from an audience, so the mind must be as fully engaged as the heart. Accordingly, writing is an imperative to speaking authentically.

Writing shows up fuzzy thinking, exposes slurred distinctions, and clarifies your position. That's why it's so difficult. Of course, it takes more time to write than to make a few notes, and time is a constant constraint for leaders. Still, it is worth doing. I am not suggesting that you must sit by a fire and compose with a quill pen; others can do the mechanics. I *am* suggesting that you must compose the *content* of what you will say, even if the words are put to paper by someone else. You must edit such drafts from your own conviction and maintain your independence from the professional. Writing your own conviction is like taking a metaphysics final in college. You can't cheat by looking into the soul of the student next to you.

Writing the speech, however, does not mean that you

have to read it to deliver it. After rehearsing the basics of the speech, you may choose to speak from notes. But "winging" a speech without a plan and written reminders of that plan results in a different message every time you speak. Writing compels consistency, and it allows the careful selection of words and phrases that will maintain your conviction and will best deliver your message to the ears of your audience. As you rehearse a written speech, you will hear its impact. You can then choose to insert more powerful words and phrases, data, and appropriate metaphors that will hold a listening audience's attention. Chapter Seven contains specific suggestion about such language.

Selecting and Working with Others

Speech counselors and advisers can be very effective, but they have to be chosen carefully. The very best speechwriters are not just good technicians but are also strong thinkers and coaches who push you to articulate your own thoughts and feelings in the most effective way. Ted Sorenson, John Kennedy's speechwriter, was also his chief of staff and conversed with the president every day. By contrast, today's speechwriters, though excellent composers, frequently have little access to their principal. They may be able to predict the position of the speaker, but they know little of the inside drive or conviction of the person for whom they write. The people you choose should be trusted associates whom you respect for more than their technical talent. They should also be willing to ask questions, offer substantive advice, listen, and then reflect *your* beliefs in impactful language.

Though Mario Cuomo is a superb writer, he includes associates in his process of composing speeches. In writing his remarks on abortion rights for the Department of Theology at the University of Notre Dame, he relied on two of his staff, both "gifted thinkers and writers, both of them profoundly Catholic and just as troubled as I was by the task of agonizing over the powerful, almost paralyzing issues raised by the abortion question. We wrote, discussed, debated, and finally decided."[5]

Others can help, but ultimately, it is your own values, your own commitment to the issue that will determine the power of the speech to you and therefore to your audience. Whatever response you as a speaker want from the audience must happen in you first. Accordingly, you must eventually hold the pen yourself and enlist only helpers who can assist you in drawing out your own conviction.

Structure: A Guide to Being Genuine

Finally, you need a framework for the speech that reflects a beginning, a middle, and an end, as well as a template of components that will serve as a checklist. This structure will channel your comments and encourage you to deliver a complete communication. The structure guides your thinking, prompting you to ask the right questions of yourself to gain access to your real conviction.

Using such a template for written speeches will also make it possible for you to be more effective when speaking extemporaneously. As you take the time and consideration to structure your comments in a way that compels you to be authentic, you will begin to convey that same conviction in other less-planned remarks. Structure will help you convey the *reason* you speak in addition to the words you say.

THE STRUCTURE OF CHANGE: THE SPEECH AS A STORY

Leadership speaking is about growth and change, words that contain a past, a present, and a future. Though it may seem terribly obvious and simplistic, a leader must keep in mind that each listener lives his or her life as a story. Despite the universal scientific evidence and our collective intuitive sense that time is an illusion, it is, as physicists say, a most *stubborn* illusion. The journey though space and time is basic in its import; it is part of the unseen atmosphere of our very existence without regard to culture. The story is to most humans like water is to the fish—so integral to existence that only our self-reflective ability allows us to see it. Everyone's life lies between some version of "once upon a time" and "they all lived happily ever after."

People resist change but embrace progress. To be committed to act, each person in the audience must have a sense of things moving forward, with the potential to make a contribution that will lead to the new future at the end of the story. So as you advocate change, you must tell us where we've been, where we are, and where we are going. Each element of the story is an opportunity for you, the speaker, to establish competence and connection with the audience.

THREE SECTIONS OF THE SPEECH: BEGINNING, MIDDLE, AND END

The purpose of the *beginning* section of a speech is to establish the speaker's credibility and to prepare the audience to listen with open minds and hearts. If you fail to accomplish these two purposes, further talk is useless. The elements of the beginning are these:

Introduction of the speaker
Acknowledgment of the audience
A concise statement of the purpose of the speech
Acknowledgment of resistance
A clear statement of the benefit of change and the
price of maintaining the status quo

The *middle* of the speech tells the story of change, elaborating the message by appealing to both the minds and the hearts of the audience. It opens the logical, emotional, and spiritual doors to gain ownership of the change in the audience. The speaker first relates the context and then discusses the reasons for the change, the steps needed to effect it, and the obstacles to it. The leader then uses data, authority, experiences, examples, metaphors, and parables to speak from both the mind and heart to the minds and hearts of the listeners.

Finally, a speech needs these elements at the *end:*

A conclusion
A call for specific action on the part of each member
of the audience
A question-and-answer session
A fresh statement of the major point of the speech

In the following chapters, we will discuss, in detail, the components of each section of the speech and the material that can best move you toward both competence and connection. I want to be clear, however, that reflection, writing, and including the elements of the template will provide only the *vehicle* for real self-expression. Following the instructions does not *guarantee* authenticity; it only makes authenticity possible. The discipline we present is like musical notation. It has form and can evoke beauty, but the real *meaning* of any musical performance can be brought forth only by the musician.

Robert Commanday, former music critic for the *San Francisco Chronicle,* illustrated this principle in a critique of a young Russian violinist, Vadim Repin, who had played Tchaikovsky's Violin Concerto in D Major with the San Francisco Symphony Orchestra. I had been in the audience, and as a former violinist, I found Repin's technique flawless. He was fast and precise and drew a standing ovation. But I had noticed only a few phrases of the music when the distinctions among instrument, violinist, orchestra, and music disappeared. As it turned out, those moments were also noticed by the critic and used as a contrast with the rest of the performance.

Commanday's critique read, in part, as follows:

> Repin has a grand, exceptionally big, warm tone, a phenomenal technique that commanded this concerto, even challenging the finale to go as vivacissimo as the orchestra can play it. Hiding somewhere underneath that there must be a personality, a musician with something to say of his own. . . . He played most of the first movement cadenza as if smoothness in bowing . . . were the principal expressive idea. [But] after the cadenza, Repin began to set off and reveal the phrases.
>
> The finale was a rouser, faster and faster, keener and keener, and the audience loved it. [But] the musicality

must develop alongside the technique and purely
violinistic mastery and be there the whole way. . . . Yes,
at 21, the essential matter is not just how he plays but
why.[6]

A master violinist's reading and playing of a musical score
does not ensure his self-expression through the instrument.
And your reading the words of the speech, even if the text
is structured perfectly, does not ensure the emergence of your
authentic voice.

Musical notation and words only *represent* the real thing.
After you have written the speech, you must deliver it from
the inside out, bringing your own internal conviction to
the symbols on the page.

The authentic speech is a continual dance between the
heart and the mind and between the speaker and the audience. Your own engagement in the subject will provide a mirror of what you are engendering in the audience. As you
are passionate, convinced, and committed about your topic,
so your audience can become passionate, convinced, and
committed. Each part of the speech gives a fresh opportunity to create such a bond.

Now we'll look at the music.

PART TWO

===

BEGINNING WELL

How to Establish Your Purpose, Competence, and Trustworthiness

▼ As in any relationship, the first few minutes set a tone that will be difficult to change. Your opening comments signal the amount of practical information your listeners can expect, the level of intimacy that you will allow, and how far you will invite them into the interaction. It is important to be aware of the impact of your words from the start. In the beginning section of the speech, you want to open the minds and hearts of the audience to hear you *and* open the door to your own deepest convictions about the subject. If you accomplish both objectives, you will maximize your chances of being authentic and thereby remove most of the causes of nervousness and self-consciousness.

The opening contains five elements: the introduction, a statement of appreciation, a statement of purpose, the acknowledgment of resistance, and a statement of the importance of the change you are advocating. Each of these elements offers an opportunity to communicate authentically.

3

TRANSFORMING CONVENTIONS INTO CONNECTIONS
Meaningful Introductions and Expressions of Appreciation

▼ Given the importance of the first impression, most speakers pay too little attention to the introduction, leaving it to the discretion of the host. Not having controlled this prelude, many spend the first few minutes adjusting the effect that has been created by the introducer. At a minimum, you can find out who will be introducing you and draft some suggested remarks. But even in the best case, you must be proactive and be ready to supplement *whatever* is said about you.

First Words: Who's Speaking?

An authentic introduction will both inform an audience about your credentials and convey some real experience of your personal qualities. Ineffective introductions include either too much or too little. It might seem nice to be introduced simply as "the president," but this simple introduction has done no service to the president of any organization or country, nor has the inane phrase "a person who needs no introduction." These introductions do not include the credentials the audience needs. Worse still are introductions (more typically heard in academic circles) that include every paper, degree, course, and credential that you have accumulated and every position you have held since graduation from secondary school. These introductions include much that is irrelevant to the topic of the speech, and the audience is left to determine what is germane. In both extreme cases, while listeners are considering whether your credentials are adequate, you have gone on with your remarks, and of course, the preoccupied audience has missed a vital part of the speech.

In the best case, the introducer will be someone familiar with you and in agreement with the change you intend to advocate. But even if you are to be introduced by someone who was merely assigned the job, you can personally design the introduction to include relevant information that will both establish your competence and begin to build an atmosphere of trust.

PRESENTING RELEVANT CREDENTIALS

Your competence to speak to a given audience on a given subject is a function of your *directly relevant* work experience, life experience, and education as well as additional credentials that might be generally important to the particular audience. Including only relevant credentials signals listeners that you consider them important.

In each culture, certain general credentials are considered fundamental to one's ability to lead. These may seem superficial, but in the early stages of a speech, before the audience has a chance to evaluate what you say or to hear your conviction on the subject, you need to establish a "foothold" of competence, just to open the audience's collective mind. In Europe, a speaker's family history, social standing, and school are generally more important than in the United States. Conversely, in America, life experience—what the speaker has done on his own—might be considered more important than his alma mater. In the Far East, credentials are often established in the process before the speech itself to avoid an introduction that is perceived as self-serving.

Audiences of specific professions will also demand different evidence to demonstrate competence. A group of academicians will indeed be interested in your education credentials, even if they are not directly related to the topic. But if you are speaking to a business audience on the value of taking risk, then work or life experience is far more valuable in establishing credibility. For example, Tom Peters's business audiences rarely discover that he holds a doctorate from Stanford. Yet when he spoke to our graduating class of M.B.A.'s at the University of California, it was an appropriate part of his introduction. Conversely, Bill Gates's or Steve Jobs's work experience is certainly adequate to establish each man's credibility, despite the fact that neither graduated from college.

MOVING TOWARD TRUST: CONVEYING PERSONAL QUALITIES

The more relevant an introduction, the more credibility you will have as a speaker. The more intimate an introduction, the closer your relationship to the audience can move toward trust. Consequently, the ideal introducer is both a friend and a professional colleague who can testify to your trustworthiness as well as your accomplishments. In such cases, you are imbued with the introducer's professional and personal reputation.

Noted psychologist Paul Kugler was introduced to a gathering of renowned archetypal psychologists in 1992 by Eugene Monick, who had attended the Zurich Institute of Jungian Psychology in Switzerland and written several books:

> I first met Paul Kugler at the Zurich Institute in the Seventies. It was later, when we were involved in the association together, that I got to know him as a colleague. He intimidated me with his capacity to intellectualize by coming at me with questions like "What do you think of Enrique's signifier of Wolfgang Giergerich's missing link of sacrifice?" or "How do you deconstruct in therapy?"
>
> Still later I roomed with Paul when we had conferences together. Sometimes three, sometimes four times a year, the association has overnights—that amounts to about eighty overnights with Paul. We became friends, and when I finally got over my intimidation (because how would you like these kinds of questions when you are walking into the shower every morning?), I found Paul to be cogent, learned, consistent, and even sometimes persuasive.
>
> Paul is a superb trainer of analysts in the life of the mind, both people who are in the training process and people who are postdiploma. He is without peer, in my mind, in his unrelenting commitment to excellence in psychological reflection.
>
> Paul's personal qualities grew on me the longer we roomed together—his kindness, his generosity, his wit.

> You are about to experience a true expert and
> wonderful man, Paul Kugler.[1]

Kugler's professional credentials were well established.
But Monick's personal reputation and his unqualified endorsement added immensely to the speaker's credibility.
Because Monick was also willing to speak from personal experience about Kugler's personal qualities, he established a
platform of trust for the speaker to stand on. This introduction needed no additions.

SUPPLEMENTING AN INTRODUCTION

If your introduction is less than ideal, you have to establish
your own credibility. Some speakers are reluctant to fill in
their own credentials, feeling that it is inappropriate to talk
about themselves. But generally, stating your credentials is
one of the greatest gifts you can give your audience and yourself. Not only does self-introduction establish a basis for the
audience's belief in what you say, but because *you* are doing
it, it can directly convey some of your personal qualities, sig-
naling an opening for trust.

Last year in San Francisco, a young professional was introduced to a business audience simply as an "environmental consultant" who would speak on the topic of "urban
conservation." He had prepared to supplement whatever was
said about him and proceeded to elaborate for the audience:

> I have been extremely fortunate to have spent most of
> my life educating myself for my work. I have spent
> almost twenty-five years in schools and over thirty years
> in the outdoors. I've traveled from the Arctic Ocean to

the Equator, climbed some of the highest peaks in
Europe, and trekked through the jungles of Borneo. As
an environmental consultant for six years, I've visited
more garbage dumps than I care to remember. I've been
involved with oil spills off the coast of Alaska and train
wrecks in densely populated urban areas. My conclusion
from all of these experiences? We are not living a
sustainable existence.

This self-introduction was not arrogant or self-serving.
It simply and colorfully let the audience know the aspects
of the speaker's education, work experience, and life experience that were relevant to the topic. Referring to himself as
"extremely fortunate" did not set him above his audience;
rather, it showed his humility and began to move him toward
a deeper connection.

In Mario Cuomo's address on abortion rights at Notre
Dame, he felt it necessary to add to his credential as governor of New York. This was a major address, given by a pro-
choice Catholic governor to the faculty of a Catholic university.
The governor knew that his political office did not establish his credibility with this audience. He added:

Let me begin this part of the effort by underscoring the
obvious. I do not speak as a theologian; I do not have
that competence. I do not speak as a philosopher; to suggest that I could would be to set a new record for false
pride. I don't presume to speak as a "good" person except
in the ontological sense of that word. . . . [Rather,] I
speak here as a politician. And also as a Catholic, a
layperson baptized and raised in the pre–Vatican II
church, educated in Catholic schools, attached to the
church first by birth, then by choice, now by love. An

old-fashioned Catholic who sins, regrets, struggles, worries, gets confused, and most of the time feels better after confession. The Catholic church is my spiritual home. My heart is there, and my hope.[2]

Aside from the beautiful words, the content of this supplementary self-introduction did far more for Cuomo's credibility with this audience than the fact that he was a governor who wrestled with public policy every day. He established his connection with this audience as a human being by including his personal motivation to speak. Despite the fact that he was advocating a very unpopular position, he was going to be trusted.

Today's cynical audiences are being asked to make radical change. They will rarely take competence for granted, even for people in positions of authority, and they will grant trust even more cautiously. An introduction that conveys relevant credentials and presents some of your personal qualities can begin to establish both.

Conveying Authentic Appreciation

Dale Carnegie anchored his systems of speaking and influencing others in the notion of sincere appreciation. Indeed, nothing connects two people like a sincere heartfelt compliment. Accordingly, most speeches begin with polite words. But if you listen carefully to the opening lines of conventional speeches, you will note how meaningless they are. "It's a pleasure to be here tonight" and "I appreciate the opportunity to speak to you" are part of an old custom that allows the speaker and audience to "settle in." These inane phrases fill in the time needed for crossing legs and folding hands. If you refuse to honor this convention, you can signal your intention to interact more authentically. I can illustrate.

In 1983, I was fortunate enough to meet with former President Jimmy Carter in Beverly Hills. My partner, Tom Green, and I were acting on behalf of some business and political leaders, promoting a very simple plan to relieve political tension between the United States and the Soviet Union. Carter had agreed to a short meeting to hear about it.

Tom and I were ushered into the suite by a Secret Service agent, and Carter entered briskly shortly thereafter. Since Tom was closer to him, he shook Carter's hand first and said something like "I am honored to meet you, Mr. President. You have been a real inspiration to me." Carter looked right at him and said, "Oh really, Tom, how's that?" I quickly ducked my head and waited for my partner to come up with something good, and in that painful ten seconds of silence that seemed like a day and a half, I learned a valuable lesson about appreciation. If it's real, it's written on your heart by experience, not on a piece of paper by convention. My partner's comment was real; he just had not reflected on *why* it was real.

Tom made a nice recovery, saying something about Carter's obvious deep partnership with Rosalyn and his courage in running for the presidency against heavy odds. When Carter shook my hand, I did not offer a gratuitous comment.

How many speakers could stand the muster of Carter's question after the conventional round of "thank yous" at the beginning of a speech? Imagine the host stopping you in the middle of such an acknowledgment and asking the Carter question—"Oh really, Tom, how's that?" By refusing to honor the convention, a speaker can establish uncommon intimacy with an audience very quickly.

FINDING REAL GRATITUDE

Authentic gratitude can be conveyed simply by reflecting on and conveying *why* you are grateful. The more specific you can be, the more you will re-create the feelings in yourself and the more authentically you will communicate them to your audience. Just that small effort can transform a mundane comment into a meaningful reflection.

I recently went through the following sequence with a corporate chairman in preparing a speech for a stockholders' meeting. He wanted to honor a board member who had attended more than fifty meetings the previous year, a particularly troubled year for the business. His first iteration read like this: "I now want to thank Mark Hubbard for his tireless support of the company in a particularly troubled year."

This certainly fits the convention. But would it stand up to the Carter question? Hardly. It would need to be enlarged with the reasons for the gratitude. "I want to thank Mark Hubbard for his tireless support of the company in a particularly troubled year. Mark attended more than fifty board and committee meetings last year, strictly out of his dedication to helping us turn the situation around. Let's give him a round of applause."

In this version, the chairman conveyed a *justification* for his acknowledgment. This rendition, even when read, began to sound like an authentic acknowledgment. But in the final revision, the chairman reflected on the *specific experiences* that gave rise to his feelings of gratefulness in the first place.

> I want to give special thanks to Mark Hubbard, who
> attended more than fifty board and committee meetings
> last year, strictly out of his dedication to helping us turn
> the situation around. I remember one such occasion,
> about seven o'clock at night in the dead of winter, when
> I was leaving my office as Mark was coming in. He had
> just finished a day at his own company, and it was
> raining, a cold rain that would turn to snow in any other
> city. He had forgotten his umbrella, so his head was
> soaked as he came into the lobby. I actually felt guilty
> leaving so early. Now it's not as though Mark doesn't
> have other interests. He came to that meeting because he
> is interested and dedicated, more as a friend of the
> company than as a board member. And he did it more
> than fifty times when we needed him most. I feel very
> lucky to have such friends serving all of us.

By reflecting on his specific experience, the chairman was
able to *find* real gratitude, not merely *talk* about it. His authenticity moved the audience with more than information. Conveying feelings that came from a real experience
made the entire episode reflect what the chairman wanted to
reflect—authentic appreciation for a friend and fellow board
member. This was hardly a perfunctory and obligatory prelude to a speech.

If appreciation is authentic, it comes from details that are
written in your memory. To access them, you don't need more
notes; you already have the experience you need. You need
only convey what happened and how you felt. This authentic appreciation signals the audience that you are willing to
engage. Rather than reading the acknowledgment, you are
recalling your gratitude. The audience *and the speaker* know
the difference.

QUESTIONS FOR AN AUTHENTIC OPENING

To enhance the opening of a speech, you can ask yourself questions that will stimulate this internal, genuine response:

> Why was I asked to speak rather than someone else?
> If I am here because of my position, what can I offer this group to humanize my authority?
> What has this group done that I admire?
> Are these people here because they have to be or because they are really interested in what I have to say?
> What do I have in common with these people, even though they might disagree with my position?
> What specific experience have I had that makes me appreciate this group or someone in it?

Your answers should yield an opening that reflects your gratefulness for the chance to address the members of this audience and your appreciation for their attention, even if they are required to be there and even if they don't agree with you.

Consider these two openings by executives addressing different institutions. Here is Robert Mahoney, chairman of Diebold, Inc., in an address at Kent State University: "Thank you for that kind introduction. It's a great pleasure to be here at Kent State University this evening. I enjoy revisiting the college setting now and then—where young minds with new ideas combine with the accumulated wisdom of past ages to pursue even greater knowledge. It kind of rejuvenates an older fellow like me."[3]

Certainly, Mahoney had given some thought to that opening. But did these remarks have any impact on the people listening to him or on his own state of mind about the speech?

Could you really tell, if you were in the audience, if he were happy to be at Kent State University?

Compare the following opening by Hilary Rodham Clinton as she addressed the American Medical Association in Chicago on the subject of health care reform:

> Thank you very much, Mr. Speaker; all of the members of the House of Delegates, the officers and trustees of the AMA and all of whom you represent. It is an honor for me to be with you at this meeting and to have the opportunity to participate with you in an ongoing conversation about our health care system and the kinds of constructive changes that we all wish to see brought to it.
>
> I know that you have, through Health Access America, and through other activities and programs of the AMA, been deeply involved in this conversation already, and all of us are grateful for your contribution. I'm also pleased that you invited students from the Nathan Davis Elementary School to join us here this afternoon. I know that the AMA has a special relationship with this school, named as it is for the founder of the AMA, and that the AMA participates in its corporate capacity in the Adopt-a-School program here in Chicago. You have made a real contribution to these young men and women. And not only have you provided free immunizations and physicals and lectures and help about health and related matters, but you have served as role models and mentors. It is very important that all of us as adults do what we can to give young people the skills they will need to become responsible and successful adults. And I congratulate you for your efforts and welcome the students here today.[4]

Though this might be standard fare for a good political speechwriter, it has the content necessary to initiate authentic gratitude. When you consider the specificity of these remarks and Clinton's expressed appreciation for the organization, it seems, at least, that she considered it important to find something to genuinely acknowledge. She thanked the organization for asking her to speak. She expressed appreciation for its work toward making "constructive changes" to the health care system. Finally, she found something very specific that the organization was doing that was important to her—working with children—and she spoke directly about her own commitment.

Imagining myself in this audience, I would feel that even given the first lady's position on health care, her opening had begun to form a bond that would be necessary for effective communication to take place. I may disagree with her, but her acknowledgment of my worth had begun to surround the interchange with a cooperative atmosphere. For Clinton, just considering and acknowledging the strength and caring of the organization allowed her to focus on the common ground. It created *in her* an attitude of respectful difference that could then set the tone for the rest of the speech.

In summary, because audiences unthinkingly honor old conventions about introductions and acknowledgment, a speaker has an excellent chance to establish himself early as different, forthright, and engaging. Such authentic expression at the outset can establish an atmosphere of openness to new ideas, even if they are unpopular.

4

ENGAGING YOUR AUDIENCE

Say What You Want Them to Change and Anticipate Resistance

▼ In his 1905 play *Man and Superman,* George Bernard Shaw connected leadership, conflict, and change with his observation that "The reasonable man adapts himself to the world; the unreasonable one persists in trying to adapt the world to himself. Therefore, all progress depends on the unreasonable man."[1] We cannot advocate change without creating conflict. But a few clients and many students are very shy about making a strong statement of purpose. By and large, they are people who were raised, like many of us, to avoid dissension. The bargain of leadership, however, is an early lack of popularity for *instigating* change in exchange for respect after *implementation* of the change. Unfortunately, these must come in sequence. If your objective is engagement and subsequent change, a strong statement of purpose is an absolute requirement. You will, in making this bargain, activate the resistance of the audience. That, too, must be dealt with authentically.

The Courage to Ask

A clear statement of purpose answers the first question of an audience, "What do you want us to do?" As a leader, you are advocating a change that you consider vital to the organization. To be authentic, you have to state your purpose strongly and explicitly at the beginning of the speech. The convention is to avoid the audience's resistance to change by hiding the purpose in clever rhetoric or by downplaying the consequences. But without a strong statement of purpose, the audience will be left asking, "So what?" University professors hear this question frequently. If you do not ask for change, people will not engage. They will be entertained or bored, but they will not engage.

The chairman of a major bank used the following statement of purpose in addressing a 1993 stockholders' meeting. The bank had been through a series of very tough audits and was in the process of recapitalization. Imagine your reaction as a stockholder hearing this: "The purpose of this meeting is to give this management team an opportunity to report on our investment and to give you every opportunity to ask questions about it. In my opening remarks, I am going to suggest substantial changes in our capitalization that may affect the value of your stock, and I don't want to leave here today with anyone unclear about the current status of the bank. Neither would I like it if anyone left here with less than *full* confidence in our ability to return the bank to profitability." The chairman realized that his plans to recapitalize the bank might well affect the stock price, and rather than hide his agenda or his point of view, he wished to engage the stockholders and allow them to engage him. Had he not been clear about his purpose, he would have risked a longer, more cynical resistance. Only by being forthright could he have a chance of trust and subsequent agreement.

Now gauge your reaction, under the same circumstances, to this more conventional opening: "The purpose of this meeting is to give this management team an opportunity to report on our investment and to give you a chance to ask questions. I'll start by describing our plans for raising money, and then each officer will report on other items of interest. We'll have plenty of time for some dialogue at the end."

The interest and engagement of an audience is a direct function of your opening statement of objective. Clarity of purpose focuses the attention of the listeners in a single direction.

N. L. Reinsch, editor of the *Journal of Business Communication,* took a similar forthright approach at a commencement address: "My remarks this morning are designed to put forward one idea. One is not a very large number. But this idea fits the occasion and merits our attention. The one idea is this: The mission of a university is to create knowledge."[2] This may not be as provocative as the opening by the bank chairman, but it is clear and concise, a statement of Reinsch's conviction that will give the speech a focused objective. Anyone in the audience who disagrees with his premise will be fully engaged. Few will be inattentive.

An advertising executive, Jim Losi, began a talk about increasing the diversity of his employee group in this way:

My topic this morning is the diversity of our employees. In the few minutes I have, I'm going to speak to the priority of this issue, the reasons for its importance, and the barriers to achieving more diversity at our company. It is not my purpose to make anyone uncomfortable, but it is my purpose to engage this group with frank and some-times personal communication, and that can make some people uncomfortable. Because this issue affects each and every one in this company, I'll leave plenty of time at the end so we can have a dialogue.

But when we are finished today, I want you to have a crystal-clear understanding of the importance of this is-sue and be ready to take some personal action to deal with it. For most of you, that will mean a change in the way you operate; but for many of you, it will also mean a change in the way you think.

Authentic decisiveness creates respect. Disagreement with a leader on an issue is offset in the minds of an audience by that leader's willingness to engage truthfully and boldly. Ac-cordingly, the more difficult the issue, the more desirable it is to state your position strongly. As a result of your strength, the audience will perceive a new boundary being created, and you will be marked as a person of principle, of strong con-viction, and of confidence.

Of course, such strong statements of advocacy will am-plify feelings of resistance in the audience and can provoke expressions of discontent. But the feelings of discontent are in the audience whether you state your purpose clearly or try to hide it in a basket of rhetoric. By shining the light on these feelings early, a speaker maintains authenticity. In fact, rec-ognizing resistance as normal gives the speaker yet another chance to connect with the hearts of the audience.

Acknowledging Resistance

Resistance is a natural response to a call for change. If you pretend that acceptance of your new proposal will come without uncertainty, you will lose credibility, risk being undermined, and never gain the full commitment of your listeners. They may *comply,* but their resistance will manifest itself in negativity and an absence of energy for the task at hand. Resistance ignored will continue to thrive, not only as the audience listens to your comments but also in the halls, highways, and homes where the audience goes to say what has not been said in your presence.

It is problematic that the people with the most resistance to your ideas will frequently avoid expressing it. Few people are willing to risk the disapproval of a leader by actually voicing doubts about his or her direction. We reveal our reservations only to people we love, respect, and trust. Accordingly, it is your responsibility to create an atmosphere that will honor dissenting views and feelings. Only by doing so can you maintain the respect and positive engagement of the audience. By acknowledging resistance, you are acknowledging reality and maintaining the aura of authenticity.

I first heard of this idea from Harvey Stone, an excellent speech coach and writer in Santa Fe, New Mexico. Harvey used the example of a domestic "discussion" in which a couple is in heated exchange, sometimes for days, until one of them acknowledges the other's feelings and opinions. Imagine yourself in a combative mood when your adversary pauses and says: "You know, I didn't realize that you felt so strongly about this issue. You sound hurt, and I know that you honestly disagree with my point of view." There is no agreement in this statement, only honest noticing and honoring of strong feelings and a different opinion. Though the discussion certainly isn't over, you can feel the energy drain out of the situation, such that ears might be open to hear for the first time in the discussion. This same release occurs when negative feelings and opinions are acknowledged in a speech. The respect for opposition voiced by the speaker can open the minds of a dissenting audience. Such acknowledgment does not *guarantee* agreement with your position, but it will dissipate the argumentative energy of the audience for the duration of the speech.

RATIONAL RESISTANCE AND CYNICISM

The easiest resistance to suspend is based on misunderstanding. The speaker simply has information that the audience does not have. The audience may be cynical about the proposed change because it has been "tried before" or may be fearful of change because of a lack of knowledge. Such resistance can be acknowledged in the beginning of the speech and actually refuted in the body of the speech.

Ned Dean, chairman of the Nestlé Beverage Company until 1992, was to speak to a group of institutional salespeople and their managers shortly after the company was consolidated. He knew that many in the institutional group were feeling as though they received less attention than the retail sales group. It was Dean's purpose to let them know that a change was needed and that he was going to make it happen. His statement of purpose activated the cynicism of this group: "I have only a short time with you, and I want to be clear up front what my purpose is. It is my intention and that of Nestlé Beverage to be number one in all markets we are engaged in. I do not want to leave this stage today until you know, beyond any doubt, that you are the most important customer we have and that we have the capability and dedication to serve you with the best quality, the most flexibility, and the greatest value of any of the Nestlé companies."

Having made this strong statement of purpose, Dean had to deal with the resistance that he had generated, the cynicism of a group that had been treated like second-class citizens. He went on to acknowledge that resistance: "Some of you might be thinking that we are too interested in retail, that you are the tail of the dog trying to wag the body. Some of you might be thinking that we are not flexible enough in our pricing, and still others might be concerned with delivery."

This statement did not, in itself, *refute* the resistance. It merely let his salespeople know that he was under no illusions about their point of view. When they realized that he knew about their doubts, they were open to hear what else he had to say. He went on to detail his specific plans to address each of their concerns.

David Craford, a sales executive with Affymetrix in California's Silicon Valley, delivered a speech advocating the acceptance and use of bioengineered food. He realized that many people were legitimately fearful of such food and acknowledged that resistance in the opening of his talk: "I know that a few of you may have some doubts about this technology—you may be afraid of putting 'bioengineered' foods into your body or having them grown in our fields. I understand these concerns. It's important for you to understand how this technology works and why we need it to work on a local and global level."

Again, Craford could not possibly eliminate all of the fears surrounding bioengineered foods. What he could do, however, was let his listeners know early that he appreciated their opinions and feelings. This opened an opportunity for them to hear his speech with their strong feelings suspended.

Resistance based on a different or inadequate understanding of the facts can be relieved with explanation. Ned Dean went on to explain his action plan to the group of institutional salespeople. David Craford explained the methods of development for "high-tech" tomatoes using common metaphors to educate his listeners and assuage their fears.

IRRATIONAL RESISTANCE

Other resistance comes not from a lack of understanding but from incorrect and entrenched beliefs. Such resistance cannot be corrected logically, and it is important for a speaker to realize this and not yield to indignation. Understanding and acknowledgment will still create an atmosphere in which the audience will listen rather than withdraw.

Consider the following comments from Charles Schwab & Co. president David Pottruck. Pottruck was also speaking on the need for more diversity in the workforce. This is a particularly emotional issue in his industry because the brokerage business has traditionally been dominated by white males. Though Schwab had a great record of moving in the right direction, the company recognized a need to accelerate its efforts even further. After introducing the subject, Pottruck made the following comments to a group of corporate managers:

> Some of you may still wonder why this topic is getting so much attention; you may still think that it is a response to government regulation or that it is *only* a moral issue that supports our values as a company. Frankly, a year ago, I might have held similar misconceptions. But after a year on the task force, reading demographics predictions, and thinking about the future of our company, I have a considerably different view.
>
> Some of you might also be threatened by the issue. If you are in the majority, you might feel that it means less opportunity or an institution of quotas. Some of you might still be under the illusion that increasing diversity will lower standards.
>
> If you see yourself as *not* a member of the majority, you might feel that the issue puts unreasonable attention on you, that you might be viewed as needing special attention, or that it is your task to educate the majority.
>
> These are understandable fears, but they are only fears. Some of them might be justified by reality. *None* of them is a reason not to move forward.

Pottruck was able, in this statement, to acknowledge the fears, respect his listeners, and challenge them to move forward anyway. Like all leadership issues, Pottruck's topic dealt with a suggested course of action to change the status quo. He is calling on others in the company for trust, asking them to progress *through* their fears to a new future. Understanding and acknowledging their resistance is another step in establishing authentic conviction about change.

Stating the Importance of Change

Obviously, to be motivated to change, an audience has to believe that the result of the change will be better than the alternative. That's why the question "Are you better off now than you were four years ago?" works so well in U.S. presidential politics. The answer to that question will indeed determine whom we vote for. The importance of change, however, is always cast in personal terms. In politics, it is up to the candidates to persuade us about the limits of our self-interest. Would we be better off with higher taxes and better schools? Should we measure "better off" with only our personal assets and earnings? The leader must clearly state the stakes of alternative choices in order to convince the public that his or her chosen course is correct. And the stakes must feel personal to the audience. Before people will act, they must feel that despite their resistance, the decision to change or not to change is personally important—that the change will make a difference to them individually.

Though you may speak about benefits and consequences in the middle of the speech, a simple statement of importance in the beginning of the speech will form the foundation for the rest of your arguments. More important, it lets the audience feel the depth of your conviction and your passion about the subject.

The Best and the Worst Case

The importance of change can be stated in the negative, in the positive, or in both ways. There is real merit in doing both, as the audience can see what you personally hope for in the future as well as what you personally dread in the status quo. Consider this 1992 statement by Warren Rudman to the U.S. Congress. Rudman, a senator from New Hampshire at the time, was speaking against the approval of the Democratic party's economic reform package. Rudman believed that the package would increase the deficit even more. Near the beginning of his speech, he commented: "In further mortgaging the future for the present, we exacerbate the very problems that got us into this mess and hamper the prospects of any real long-term recovery." This statement became the launchpad for his appeal.

It is unlikely that any speech on the floor of the United States Senate sways senatorial votes. But this speech was also heard by many in the American public and was later published in the congressional record. To capture the imagination, to gain a hearing for the advocacy of painful change, a speaker needs to present both the best-case and the worst-case scenario.

Rudman has been a champion of fiscal responsibility for decades and clearly sees the positive aspects of restraint. He could have added the optimistic scenario and been more effective—for example: "In further mortgaging the future for the present, we exacerbate the very problems that got us into this mess and hamper the prospects of any real long-term recovery. *But if we avoid further charges to our unlimited credit card, we could actually reverse the trend of rabid deficit growth and create prosperity for our children that is built on fiscal integrity rather than self-indulgence.*"

Hearing this possibility of a positive future lets the audience know that the speaker is not merely a naysayer, even if the speech is advocating a negative action. It signals the audience that the leader has reflected on the issue itself, has measured it against personal values, and has found positive consequences in an alternative. This leader is then worth taking seriously.

The following sequence was spoken by Anita Roddick, managing director of The Body Shop International at the 1993 Congress of the International Chamber of Commerce. An advocate for corporate responsibility, she stated her purpose as follows: "We want a new paradigm, a whole new framework, for seeing and understanding [that] business can and must be a force for positive social change. It must not only avoid hideous evil . . . it must actively do good."[3]

After describing only a few instances of exploitation, Roddick told the audience the stakes:

> Now if this blind pursuit of licentious trade continues, political instability will return big time. The rise of fascism, brutal nationalism, and the ethnic racism we see on continent after continent are no accident.
>
> Demagogues *prey* on insecurity and fear; they breed in the darkness of poverty and desolation. If we do not build an economic growth that helps sustain communities, cultures, and families, the consequences will be severe. Even if our politics somehow survives, our globe will not.[4]

Is this hyperbole? Not to Roddick. The passion she expresses with these words reveals an authentic concern with the current course of world trade. Her statement of the importance of change gives notice of the strength of the speech that follows.

Though I consider her entire speech brilliantly done, had

I been in the audience, I would have felt a little browbeaten in the beginning. Had she added a positive scenario, I would have seen a new possibility, a chance for redemption, and would have been glued to her suggestions on how to reverse this trend—for example: *"But if we truly take responsibility for our businesses, if we see that our long-term economic interests will be served by developing communities rather than exploiting them, we can be what politics has never become: a force that actually changes peoples' lives for the better. And we can all get rich in the process, economically as well as spiritually."*

This idea can certainly be gleaned from the speech as a whole, but an early statement of the positive possibilities of change puts the audience on notice, establishes a foundation for the rest of the speech, and firmly reveals the alternatives that the leader authentically perceives.

In the beginning of the speech, the speaker sets the tone and the limits for the audience, inviting them to entertain change. The degree of both confidence and trust that develops between you and your audience will be determined by the authenticity you can transmit. The style of your introduction, the way in which you show appreciation for your listeners, the strength of your purpose, the empathy you portray for their resistance, and the cost and benefit they perceive in your advocacy—each of these elements will affect their willingness to continue to listen.

After you have included these rudiments, it is time to tell your story.

PART THREE

—

TELLING THE WHOLE STORY

How to Inspire Commitment to Change

▼ We began by defining the leader as a person who sees what is needed and then inspires others to take action to effect change. We further observed that implicit in change is a past, a present, and a future—the way it was, the way it is, and the way it will be.

Most people don't view issues broadly enough to recognize that they have become more or less important over time. Neither do most of us consider issues in relationship to other issues. We tend to view each change as insular, as not affecting other aspects of our lives. In speaking about the need for change, you, as a leader, are relating your rendition of the past, present, and future of the issue as well as enlarging the perspective of the audience about the ripple effects of change. You are compelling your listeners to agree with your larger and longer view. This accord is crucial because different versions of the story will lead to different conclusions and hence to different opinions and feelings about what kind of change is needed.

As of this writing, the health care debate in the United States is being conducted primarily on the basis of various versions of our nation's health care story. What was our system like in the past? What has changed to render portions of the system inefficient? What is the real current state of our health care system? What is the most appropriate vision for the future of the system? What is the "right" thing to do? Each leader has a different view of the story. Whoever persuades the majority of the public that his or her point of view is the most accurate will enlist enough followers to effect change. The successful leader will gain full agreement about the *context* of the issue.

The need for shared context is the same in any organization. In a family, parents and their children rarely perceive the same context. Hence the constant question from the child: "Why?" In business, employees often greet changes in market needs and shifts in organizational structure with the phrase "I don't understand why we are doing this." The question "Why?" is a request for the story. The answer to the question provides *meaning* for the action being taken.

As these examples illustrate, to win followers, you must transmit not only information but also the subjective basis of your conviction. "Because I said so" will not win commitment. You must offer credibility and trustworthiness, evidence and passion, facts and faith. In the words of James Kouzes and Barry Posner, "Leaders are like mediums—they act as channels of expression between down-to-earth followers and their other-worldly dreams."[1] When listeners agree with your story, they see, feel, and understand the need for change. And in an age of discontinuity, an age when the past does not logically predict the future, it is even more critical that you build a substantial bridge between what was and what needs to be.

In the beginning of the speech, you have taken a great deal of time to prepare yourself and your audience. As you now establish the context of the change and articulate the consequences, benefits, and barriers, your time will be limited by the attention span of the audience and by the edges of your own enthusiasm to deliver details. The evidence you offer should be restricted to a few powerful pieces that appeal to both the minds and the hearts of the audience. To remain authentic, you must choose evidence that appeals to your own mind and heart as well. The middle of the speech contains the message, and each time you give the speech, you must also receive the message again, right along with the audience.

In the chapters in Part Three, you will see how to tell the story of change simply and authentically, fully developing the context and using evidence that is the most compelling to *you*. We will also explore ways to use language to spark the imagination of your audience.

5

BUILDING SHARED CONTEXT

Make the Change Meaningful

▼ Many speeches are all context. Authorities are often asked merely to explain why something is true. These experts will then speak on the economy, the company marketing strategy, or the history of the church. Their purpose is not to advocate change. Their purpose is to inform, to explain the background, and to give the audience a base of knowledge.

For a leader advocating change, however, context plays two major roles. It is the circumstances in which the change will occur—the story—and also the part of a passage that surrounds a particularly powerful statement. As the accumulation of information accelerates, context become paramount to understanding. It is absolutely essential to authenticity in that it determines the meaning, either of the speaker's entire position or of a single statement.

Context as Story

As you tell the story of the circumstances that led to the need for change, you are accomplishing two purposes. First, you are establishing a common understanding of events leading up to the status quo. This common understanding becomes the foundation for a decision to change. Second, you are presenting a view of the issue that is broader than the self-interest of the audience and large enough to hold the change you are advocating. You are offering your listeners a chance to be a part of something unchangeable and something larger than themselves.

A COMMON UNDERSTANDING

When an audience and the leader agree on the context, change is a natural outcome. The current behavior or method of doing things is seen as part of an old and ineffective pattern. When agreement occurs, the old pattern is abandoned to reflect the new reality.

The world of baseball gave us a solid lesson in the significance of context during one of the pastime's most famous games. Fans get chills at the mention of a perfect game. "Perfect" here means that the pitcher has been successful in getting every batter on the opposing team out three times in nine innings. Not one player from the other team reaches first base. A perfect game is a very rare occurrence.

Only one such game has ever been pitched in the World Series of baseball. Stephen Jay Gould, natural scientist and author, related the story in the *New York Times* and later his collection of essays, *The Flamingo's Smile:*

What could be more elusive than perfection? And what would you rather be . . . the agent or the judge? Babe Pinelli (who died at age 89 in a convalescent home near San Francisco) was the umpire in baseball's unique episode of perfection when it mattered most. October 8, 1956. A perfect game in the World Series . . . and, coincidentally, Pinelli's last official game as arbiter. What a consummate swan song. Twenty-seven men to the plate, and twenty-seven men down. And since single acts of greatness are intrinsic spurs to democracy, the agent was a competent but otherwise undistinguished Yankee pitcher, Don Larsen.

The dramatic end was all Pinelli's, and controversial ever since. Dale Mitchell, pinch hitting for Sal Maglie, was the twenty-seventh batter. With a count of 1 ball and 2 strikes, Larsen delivered one high and outside . . . close, but surely not, by its technical definition, a strike. Mitchell let the pitch go by, but Pinelli didn't hesitate. Up went the right arm for called strike three. Out went Yogi Berra from behind the plate, nearly tackling Larsen in a frontal jump of joy. "Outside by a foot," groused Mitchell later. He exaggerated . . . for it was outside by only a few inches . . . but he was right.

Babe Pinelli, however, was more right. A batter may not take a close pitch with so much on the line. *Context matters.* Truth is a circumstance, not a spot.

Truth is inflexible. Truth is inviolable. By long and recognized custom, by any concept of justice, Dale Mitchell had to swing at anything close. It was a strike . . . a strike high and outside. Babe Pinelli, umpiring his last game, ended with his finest, his most perceptive, his most truthful moment. Babe Pinelli, arbiter of history, walked into the locker room and cried.[1]

Babe Pinelli was able to break the rules by virtue of the universally understood context of the game of baseball and the circumstances of this particular game. Had the game been played at midseason, with nothing on the line, he would have called the pitch a ball—or, had he called a strike, there would have been cries of "We were robbed!" In this case, in this context, the leader stated the truth, and the change was agreed to instantly by everyone in the park, by everyone who was glued to a radio, and, I would bet, even by Dale Mitchell.

Common understanding of the context creates a justification to break old rules in favor of doing the right thing, something that is needed with every change we make. In the case of the imperfect strike, every baseball fan in America understood the context and agreed to the change in the rules.

Unfortunately, in the games of world business and geopolitics, galloping instability prevents many players from knowing the context and thereby determining the value of change. Accordingly, very few people are willing to commit to change without a substantial education. The leader has to inform them of the context and then remind them, again and again. If you do not do so, your suggested change will be perceived as meaningless.

I was on a trip to the Far East when an aspiring Japanese M.B.A. candidate engaged me in conversation at Japan's First Bank of Commerce. We had just heard a lecture about the changing relationship between Japanese banks and their customers. The young man explained to me that for the past fifty years, Japanese banks and their commercial business customers were partners with the Japanese government. The incentives for industry and financial service entities had been clearly the same over that period. Regulations, however, were now changing to give banks and the commercial customers they serve some different motivations. Accordingly, customers are no longer willing to accept the judgment of the bank without question. For the first time, the bank was being asked by customers to justify currency trades made on their behalf that turned out badly. In the absence of common goals, customers need to know why banks make these currency trades. To respond, the bank started a series of training classes for their customers to explain the vagaries of currency trading. They took the responsibility of articulating the context for their customers.

Later in the same conversation, the young man told me that the identical problem exists between the older generation in the bank and his own peers. "The veterans have the benefit of the old culture, and we do not. Consequently, we do not understand the reason for their actions." This contextual misunderstanding was grounded in something far greater than the reasons for making certain trades. In this case, the leaders of the bank had not shared the context of the historical linkages among banks, their longtime customers, and the government. Such connections run very deep and are based on the fundamental pillars of the interconnected Japanese culture and economy. Because this young man and others like him had gone to school in the West, they were unfamiliar with these roots. The reason that the young man was seeking was based on unspoken understandings of the past and their consequences in the present, a connection that was not communicated by his elders.

By explaining the *why* of currency trading to its customers, this bank ensured the continued loyalty of its customers. But without the *why* of the Japanese business culture, young

Japanese employees will perform their duties without meaning and without ever developing any loyalty to the institution.

In preparing a speech advocating change, the leader considers the background, examining the history of the issue, thinking through the broad implications of change, and, ideally, reflecting on the moral consequences. Listeners, however, have not looked at the issue so thoroughly; they have not traced the issue to its conclusion, nor have they examined the history leading up to change. Like the Japanese student, they do not have the benefit of seeing the issue against the background of the old culture. A leader provides that perspective by communicating such knowledge to them.

Richard Rosenberg, chairman and CEO of BankAmerica Corporation, advocated three management practices to the Executive Club of Chicago in May 1993. After a rather good opening about the difficulty of looking to the future, Rosenberg began the context of his remarks:

> It always helps when contemplating the future to look
> briefly back at the past. Does anybody here remember
> what they were doing on October 4, 1957? That was
> roughly 35 years ago, well within many of our working
> lifetimes. It was the day that the Soviet Union launched
> *Sputnik,* which many historians say was the symbolic
> transition from the industrial age to the information
> age—a time when the value of the human mind began to
> eclipse the value of natural resources.
>
> On October 4, 1957, the top 10 businesses in
> Chicago were Swift, Standard Oil, Armour, International
> Harvester, Inland Steel, Wilson, Sears, Montgomery
> Ward, Prudential Insurance and the First National Bank
> . of Chicago.

Thirty-five years later, the list of Chicago's top businesses, ranked by sales, is a little different. It still includes Sears and First National, but it also includes CNA Financial, AMOCO, Continental Bank, Citicorp Diner's Club, and Commonwealth Edison.

But ranked by market capitalization—which many would agree is a more meaningful measure—Chicago's biggest companies include Ameritech, Abbott Labs, McDonald's, Motorola, Waste Management, and Baxter.

These lists dramatically illustrate the evolution that American business has gone through over the past 35 years—an evolution characterized by a move away from commodities and commodity-type manufacturing to financial services, health care, and technology in many different formats.

The lists also lead to the next question: Which companies will be among the top 10 in the next 35 years?[2]

Rosenberg uses history to create the context for the audience and determine the meaning of his remarks that follow. What will be the measure of the change he will advocate? The makeup of the top ten businesses in Chicago thirty-five years from now. He has successfully told this audience "where we have been" and "where we are."

John Adams, chairman and CEO of the Texas Commerce Bank, spoke to the National Council of Jewish Women in 1993 about juggling job and family. His purpose was to deliver the message to corporate leaders (the speech was published) that employees—women employees in particular—needed to be encouraged to pay attention to their families and should be accommodated rather than placed under more pressure to increase their time at work. After stating the purpose, Adams went on to ask the contextual question explicitly:

> Why are corporate leaders more and more addressing work-family issues in their business planning and management?
>
> One obvious reason is the changing family. When the drive to American industrial dominance began to build steam in the '50s, the country was comfortable with the notion of a working husband and a wife at home with kids. It made sense in the wake of World War II. The men had come home. Rosie the Riveter could leave the factory. They both wanted children, and American prosperity enabled single-earner families to lead comfortable lives.
>
> Today, we must deal with new realities. Remember the guy who wouldn't dream of his wife working? He's the same guy who now wakes her up in the middle of the night to suggest that she ask her boss for a raise.
>
> Fewer than 22 percent of married-couple households consists of a male breadwinner and female homemaker. In the 1950s, the figure was 80 percent.
>
> Fifty-eight percent of mothers with children under six now hold paying jobs. The figure was 20 percent in 1960. And 68 percent of mothers with children under 18 work outside the home.
>
> Today, the majority of families rely on two incomes to maintain a middle-class standard of living, and a significant number of families need two incomes just to pull themselves above the poverty line. Two working parents, and single parents, bring an array of needs with them into the workforce that didn't exist before.[3]

This is context well done. There is no question that the members of this audience have a firm grasp on the value of the issue, its relationship to other issues, and the history of the issue. Adams has told them "where we have been" and "where we are" and has let them know why we need to break the established rules of work. He has forged a solid connection, established a common context, and laid the groundwork for promoting his advocacy to a listening audience.

VALUES THAT ARE LARGER THAN SELF-INTEREST

A second aspect of context is that it establishes a broader perspective of the *value* of change. Peter Senge, in researching *The Fifth Discipline,* found that a profound sense of scale was common to inspirational leaders. Each leader, says Senge, "perceived a deep story and sense of purpose that lay behind his vision, what we have come to call the *purpose story*— a larger 'pattern of becoming' that gives unique meaning to his personal aspirations and his hopes for their organization."[4] Senge suggests that reflection on your own personal values will yield a broader and more personal context for your role as leader. Communicating this larger purpose story invites listeners to become a part of something larger than themselves, giving them a chance to make a difference in a bigger arena than they have perceived possible. You are giving your audience the opportunity to trade commitment for greatness. Nearly all find this a very good bargain.

Consider John Sculley's dream for Apple. "We just want to change the world," said Sculley. "It seems like a lot to do, but if you're going to dream, you might as well dream big." Or consider the fact that Stephen Hawking's first book, *A Brief History of Time,* has sold nearly six million copies in thirty languages since its publication in 1989—astounding when you consider that according to the author, to read and understand this book (an explanation of the search for a unifying theory for the origin and working of the universe) would qualify the reader to start a Ph.D. in theoretical physics. Many explanations have been offered for the book's unanticipated popularity. Hawking, however, thinks the reason is simply that the general public wants to be involved in the discussion of "really big questions."[5]

I agree. Many leaders, in all fields, are too quick to patronize their public, assuming that people are selfish, dull, or uninterested in global or universal questions. Quite the contrary, the public is eager to hear, eager to engage, and eager to act when called to contribute to just causes that are larger than themselves. All monumental changes that eventually occur originally seem to be *too* great, *too* challenging, *too* costly. The reformation of the Christian church, the creation of the United States, the freeing of slaves in America, the flight to the moon, the reunification of Germany— all of these great changes seemed beyond reach. Yet each one was accomplished by ordinary people sharing the vision of a leader. The cynicism of today's audiences can be weakened by a speaker who can present change as a chance for others to have an impact on a scale that is much larger than the immediate and obvious.

Anita Roddick established the following context in her speech to the International Chamber of Commerce:

> There is always someplace in the world that is a little
> worse off, where the living conditions are a little more

wretched. Just look at industry after industry in search of even lower wages and looser standards. From Europe or the U.S. to Taiwan to Malaysia. Each country is just another pit stop in the race to the bottom. The new frontier is China, where wages and environmental standards are still lower and human rights abuses even more sordidly suppressed. The new nomadic capital never sets down roots, never builds communities; it leaves behind toxic wastes and embittered workers.

You may think this is hyperbole. Please go out and check. Visit the cities capital flight has left behind in the U.S. and England. Go to the places I have been around the world where capital has newly—and temporarily—alighted. Hold the mutated babies, genetically handicapped by toxic wastes dumped in local streams. Meet the indigenous communities being driven out of existence.[6]

Roddick has produced a marvelous context. We see *her* story of the global cost of a capitalist free-for-all and *her* experience of the broad negative impact of trade unrestricted by care for human values. The members of the audience are called to change things that are larger than their own short-term interest.

An appeal to values taps the humanity of your audience. If the change you want will legitimately make life better for others, your audience will respond, whether you are asking for better customer service or assistance to the poor.

As historical and philosophical background, context creates the meaning for change. The past and present of the issue form the foundation for agreement about the future, and enlarging the scale of the issue can inspire the audience to contribute to a grander cause.

Context as the Meaning for "Sound Bites"

But context is more than the history and scope of the issue. It also forms the background of individual statements and in doing so gives power to your most substantive points. Without context, such points lack the resonance to be remembered. In the evidentiary part of the speech, context plays this second role, to surround and give meaning to a particularly powerful summary statement. Without context, such an assertion is often referred to as a "sound bite," a short, catchy saying developed solely as a headline or a fleeting television news clip.

The increasing use of sound bites reflects the spiraling demands of the media and the escalating use of marketing professionals in all of communication. It is part of our "hurry-up" society. In *Care of the Soul,* Thomas Moore describes the extensive use of sound bites as "symptomatic of a superficial approach to life, wanting information like fast food, taking it in quickly without substance, rather than absorbing life, digesting it, and making it part of us. Such truncated communication is not authentic. It is devoid of any evidence of reflection or consideration of its impact on the listener."[7]

In business, the sound bite without context is the vision or mission statement that is developed by a consultant, engraved on a plaque, and put on every employee's wall. It is indeed like fast food, prepared by someone else and presented in one flavor. Without a context of involvement in the process of developing the statement, employees see such statements as meaningless fluff.

However, when clothed in context, these short, headline-type phrases can provide instant recall of a set of ideas or instant re-creation of a set of feelings. Sound bites can create a link to shared meaning without the need to repeat the context. Advertising companies do this by inventing slogans and imbuing them with meaning, showing images of good things happening as the slogans are read or displayed. These background images create the context of shared meaning between the advertiser and the audience. "You've got the right one, baby," "It's the real thing," "Just do it," "Maybe it's time for Schwab"—these catchphrases bring back the memory of images in the advertisements, images that are positive and compelling. Without images or context, the slogans would be meaningless. In strictly oral communication, it is necessary for the speaker to build context before the sound bite can create any substantial connection.

It is in the field of public service that context is needed most and offered least. The needs of the media for short, concise nine-second sound bites have been dictating what politicians say, and few seem to have made the distinction between the requirements of the media and those of the electorate. Consequently, when running for office, politicians address multiple issues in one speech, and that habit frequently continues after they are elected. It is almost impossible to include adequate context on eight issues in a thirty-minute speech, so few even try. The result is a series of one-liners, all suitable as headlines or sound bites. The practice has become so common that many of the most important speeches that political leaders make contain lots of glib words and little meaning.

President Bill Clinton gave us an example of a naked sound bite in his inaugural address in 1993. Although a fine speech overall, the president delivered one memorable line that was aching for context and could have been the high point of the speech. "There is nothing wrong with America that cannot be cured by what is right with America" came from his lips after only one introductory line. Here is the full passage: "Our democracy must be not only the envy of the world but the engine of our own renewal. There is nothing wrong with America that cannot be cured by what is right with America. And so today we pledge an end to the era of deadlock and drift, and a new season of American renewal has begun."

This was one of the fundamental themes of the speech and, indeed, of his entire presidential campaign. The richness of this idea would have provided a powerful connection with the American people had it been related to a context. Let me suggest the following:

> Our democracy will not only be the envy of the world, but it will also continue to be the engine of our own renewal.
>
> We hear talk about the education problem in the United States, yet there are thousands of teachers who are truly dedicated, who stay up grading papers, and who call parents regularly. There are parents who both work and yet somehow manage to go to the parent meetings at the school and help their own children with homework.
>
> We hear of the trade deficit or unemployment, yet there are men and women who own small businesses who constantly work seventy-hour weeks to make their products more competitive in foreign markets; and there are technicians who labor at night making innovative breakthroughs for the next generation of technology.
>
> And we hear of the drug problems, yet there are people in neighborhoods all over the country who are standing guard at the corners or patrolling the parks or using

the courts to get landlords to close down crack houses. There are beat police officers who are helping ordinary folks get their streets back.

This is the heart of our country.

There is nothing wrong with America that can't be cured by what is right with America.

Putting the statements of what is *wrong* against the background of what is *right* would have taken one additional minute, yet it would have meant the difference between an audience connection and a rhetorical trick.

Authentic speaking requires reflection on the meaning of each assertion. Without such reflection, sound bites become little more than pontification. But by wrapping these strong phrases in the context of evidence, you can transform them into a memorable shorthand for shared meaning.

The Rest of the Story: Confirming Trust and Confidence

The historical context can be seen as one side of the chasm. On the other side of the chasm is the future. Once you and the audience agree about the context, you have also agreed on the need for change. But to jump this chasm with you, the audience must be convinced of your competence and satisfied that you are trustworthy. The rest of the message addresses both of these issues.

The question of competence is objective and will take the form of objective questions:

Is the change you are advocating the best alternative?
What are the benefits of taking the action you are suggesting?
What are the consequences if we don't change?

What are the barriers to change?
What steps do we need to take?

These concerns will be answered with logical and concrete evidence.

The question of your trustworthiness, however, is subjective. It will be answered in the personal experiences, analogy, metaphors, and stories that you use to support your own authenticity.

I visited Singapore early in 1994 with a group of students from the University of California. Near the waterfront in a downtown bank plaza is a Salvador Dali bronze, *Homage to Newton,* which stands fifteen feet high. *Newton* is an abstract figure of a human featuring large holes in the skull and chest. A bronze heart is suspended from a fine wire in the center of the body, and a brain is carved to appear suspended in the skull. A plaque states that it is by expressing both mind and heart that all of human enterprise is accomplished. This is indeed the challenge of today's leaders. Inspiring committed action requires appealing to both the heart and the mind. Both purpose (what will be accomplished) and meaning (why we want to accomplish it) are required to engage others fully.

Blaise Pascal, the seventeenth-century mathematician, had a running argument with René Descartes about Descartes's axiom "I think, therefore I am." The conflict was often bitter, but when Pascal became ill, Descartes attended him as a physician and stayed with him for long periods of time. When Pascal asked about his reason for staying with and caring for such a longtime rival, Descartes replied, "The heart has reasons that reason knows nothing of."[8]

But to many leaders, particularly those trained as lawyers

or business professionals, this center section of the speech is where one "proves" the case. Particularly in Western culture, such proof is considered sacrosanct, and an audience that ignores it is considered either incapable of grasping the truth or irresponsible. Yet each day we see juries making decisions that seem to be totally unjustified by the facts of the case. In reality, they have looked for holes in the judge's instructions that will allow them to return a verdict consistent with the direction in which their hearts are leading them. To ignore this phenomenon, to disregard our ability and desire to enlarge our experience of life to include the facts and move beyond them, is to fail to lead.

The jury is merely the most obvious case of proof not necessarily dictating action. There are others:

> Very logical public policy decisions fail in implementation because the people at the grassroots operate more on feelings than logic and refuse to change the level of assistance to those they help.
>
> Decisions by corporate executives, steeped in logic, don't get carried out at the operational level because employees don't really care about the success of the company.

During a 1993–1994 "reengineering," Nynex executive vice president Bob Thrasher made three board presentations on three consecutive days—what he called "the most excruciating days of my life." He asked these boards to make fundamental changes to the company that would eliminate thousands of jobs. Showing slides of expected results, he predicted an internal return of 1,025 percent and a payback on investment in two years, despite the estimated implementation cost of $1.6 billion. Commenting on the process, Thrasher says, "Some of our managers still don't get it. What we've got to do is find them and get them out of the business."[9]

I'm sure all of the managers "got it"—that is, they understood exactly what was needed. I'm sure, too, that they were confident of Thrasher's competence to get it done. Why, then, did his wishes not get carried out by these managers?

Cynicism has led people to acknowledge new ways of deciding. We are not willing merely to connect the dots to form the picture; we want to draw outside of the lines of the strategic mind.

Competence is necessary, but insufficient, to gain commitment from an audience. The mind makes a decision based on agreement with the information the speaker provides. The heart makes the commitment based on a feeling of connection to the leader.

The mind looks for evidence; the heart looks for passion. The mind weighs facts; the heart acts on faith. The mind looks for purpose; the heart seeks meaning. The mind believes; the heart trusts.

In the next two chapters, we will explore how you can chose and communicate your supporting material to gain the full commitment of the audience.

6

WINNING PEOPLE'S MINDS

Offer the Right Supporting Evidence

▼ Evidence to support a given point of view is abundant, and leaders no longer have privileged access to that evidence. Clearly, the amount of information to be known is accelerating at a rate substantially faster than anyone's ability to know it, and accessing that information is becoming easier. The world's public, even in the most remote regions, has a wealth of data available.

My older son was in Central America in the Peace Corps in the early 1990s. He would often spend a night in a jungle village without electricity, and the next night, only twenty miles away, he would watch live cable television from the United States. Soon, even the jungle will give way to the march of information. CNN takes live footage of invasions, and reporters interview "enemies" at home in their living rooms. The equivalent of an M.B.A. education is available on late-night television in most major media markets in the United States. Politicians and business leaders speak to us directly on C-SPAN, and radio talk-show hosts "educate" everyone from the janitorial staff to those in the boardroom. The Internet shrinks the world yet another size. Regardless of whether all of this information is accurate, its availability gives any audience a new reference point to measure the competence of anyone who speaks.

Brevity and Simplicity

Clearly, then, the bridge to credibility and trust is supported more by the strength of the connection than by the number of reasons a leader can supply for the change. Yet just as authors often believe that they must put all of their accumulated knowledge in their first book, leaders often think it is important to be comprehensive in a speech that advocates a new direction. We perceive that the more radical the change, the more extensive the speech must be and the more the transformation must be rationalized. This is a fallacy.

Appeals for change should be brief, never longer than forty-five minutes. Lasting acceptance of substantial change comes gradually, so audiences need to hear such proposals in short, clear narratives. Familiarity with the old way, the perceived risk of the new situation, leaving real and symbolic friends—these considerations will be eroded slowly. Given the time we need to incorporate change psychologically, emotionally, and spiritually, a long and comprehensive first appeal, even by a good speaker, can be counterproductive.

Likewise, keeping the logical structure of the speech simple allows you to speak with fewer references to notes; more important, it makes it possible for the audience to retain the points that you do make. A preview, in which you create a verbal list for the audience, helps keep you and the audience on track and can aid in maintaining attention—for example, "Now that we know the stakes of this change and understand the history and scope of the issue, I want to look briefly at the three most formidable barriers to making this change. Then I'll suggest the steps we have to take together. We'll have time for questions at the end."

Or consider this alternative: "I think we agree on how we got here. I'll spend the next fifteen minutes discussing the benefits of moving forward and the consequences that I see if we don't. I won't pretend to answer all of the questions that will be in your minds tonight, but you will have a chance to ask them all in the next few days and weeks."

The Effective Use of Data

Now it's time for proof. You must display your competence to make logical judgments through effective communication of relevant data, authorities, examples, and other factual evidence. Such objective validation appeals to the minds of audience members, convincing them that the change would be a "good idea." Because the audience hears so much conflicting data, you must use care in your choice and display of evidence.

SPECIFICS TO ENCOURAGE ENGAGEMENT

We equate specificity with certainty, so precise evidence is far more powerful than generalities. When evidence is specific, it allows comparison and judgment, engaging listeners in a mental process rather than treating them as passive receptors.

Al Clausi, president of the Institute of Food Technologists, addressed the National Institute of Standards and Technology Conference in 1994. The audience was composed of people who understood and appreciated the use of statistics. Clausi's purpose was to implore the delegates to institute a change in public policy to support the research needs of the food industry. He began by stating, "I will now assert that *food* is the fabric of America. Food fuels not only our appetites but [also] our economy."

To support this assertion, Clausi added quickly, "I don't want to spend much time talking numbers. But one minute's worth will describe the scope of our enterprise. Food is our nation's largest manufacturing sector. The annual value of shipments by the nation's 16,000 food manufacturers (1987 [industry] census) approaches $400 billion. Adding value to raw farm commodities, by processing them into foods, employs 1.5 million Americans. In 1991 we contributed $145 billion in 'added value' to our domestic economy. That compares with chemicals, including pharmaceutical, [which] contributed $155 billion, and transportation equipment, including cars, [which] contributed $152 billion. Enough numbers."

Later, as he spoke of the need to promote health and safety in foods, he commented: "If improved nutrition reduced health care costs by 10 percent . . . a realistic goal . . . the savings to the country would be $14.6 billion."[1]

These data were specific and therefore engaging and effective. The comparison of the food industry to others that were known by the audience (drugs and cars) also provided a meaningful comparative for the statistics.

Note your reaction to these same thoughts if only generalities were used: *"I don't want to spend much time talking numbers. It is sufficient to say that the nation's food manufac-*

turing sector is huge. It compares favorably with the chemical and transportation industries in its size and impact on American jobs and GDP." And later: *"If improved nutrition reduced health care costs by a few percentage points, the results would be impressive."*

The difference is apparent. Specificity enhances the authority of any speaker. It provides evidence that you have paid close attention to the issue rather than merely read a briefing book.

INCLUDING THE AUDIENCE

But because each member of an audience is judging the supporting material from a personal point of view, maintaining your connection requires that you relate objective evidence to your listeners directly. Choosing evidence that will show the impact on your audience is the first challenge. Making sure that the audience realizes that impact is the second.

In a speech to the Oil and Gas Conference in Houston, James Paul, president of the Coastal Corporation, wanted to impress his listeners with the fact that there was waste in government. He also wanted them to hear how this waste was affecting them directly: ". . . It's even a greater national disgrace when 15 years' worth of tax cuts result in everyone actually paying more taxes than before. And what do those dollars buy? *You,* as a taxpayer, paid $370,000 to kick off Smokey the Bear's 50th anniversary celebration. *You* paid $2.7 million for a catfish farm. *You* paid $219,000 to teach college students how to watch television. . . . *You* even paid $144,000 to see if pigeons follow human economic laws!"[2]

Paul included the audience simply by emphasizing the

word *you*. He could have said "our government," but by emphasizing *you*, he was able to connect with his audience as individuals, not just as members of the same legal jurisdiction.

DRAWING CONCLUSIONS

Frequently, the relationship of the data presented is unclear to the audience. Rather than letting listeners struggle with relevance, tell them straight out what the information means.

At my younger son's university graduation in 1994, the chancellor took his obligatory turn at the microphone and used ten minutes to encourage our financial support of higher education. He used data to substantiate the excellence of the school, naming the number of Nobel laureates on the faculty and the amount of research money they were able to attract. He used statistics, comparing the amount of research money procured by the university to like numbers from other top universities in the United States.

It was interesting but not engaging. As I surveyed the audience of students and parents with my speech critic's eye, I could see that the level of attention was due to the audience's pride in accomplishment, not anything that was being said.

Then the chancellor began to discuss the increased competition to gain admission to the university that had resulted from its enhanced reputation. He quoted the minimum combination of SAT score and grade point average required for admission four years previously and compared it to the same standard today. It was much tougher to gain admission today than it had been in previous years, he averred. "This means if you look to your left and your right, one of the two people you see, your fellow graduates, would not be admitted to this institution if they were applying today."

The atmosphere in the audience immediately changed. The chancellor had made it possible for each person to experience the relevance of the data directly. As I was listening and watching the students look right and left, I was also wondering if my son would have been one of those who would still gain admission. My mind immediately made the data personal, and as a result, I felt a much closer connection to the statistics and to the speech.

GLOBAL DATA MADE LOCAL

Another effective way of making data relevant is to express them in terms of a familiar setting. If the evidence is global or from a context that is not familiar to the audience, the numbers can be cast against a more commonplace background.

Timothy Wirth, assistant secretary of state, used this technique in speaking to the National Press Club in Washington, D.C., in 1994. His topic was global conditions. He quoted statistics about the loss of farmland in China: "In China, home to one in five of the earth's people, severe water shortages and soil erosion threaten that nation's ability to sustain its population. Between 1957 and 1990, China lost nearly 70 million acres of cropland, an area the size of all the farms in France, Germany, Denmark, and the Netherlands combined."[3]

Wirth expressed the data in a setting (western Europe) that was more familiar to his audience than China. Given that his audience was made up exclusively of Americans, he could have been even more effective had he related the loss in China to a land area in the United States—for example, South Dakota, Nebraska, and Kansas.

Statistics are essential to the justification for change. However, they can be communicated in a way that includes listeners, encourages their interaction with the data, and adds to their respect and trust for the speaker.

Quotations from Authorities

Quoting an authority who agrees with your ideas can not only add considerable weight to your evidence but also deepen your connection with the audience. But done without reflection, it can also *damage* both aspects of your credibility. For example, it is a common mistake to quote a philosopher, academic, or other expert without really knowing the person's work or, even worse, to quote a person whom listeners do not know, leaving them baffled and wondering about their own intelligence. This can make you seem arrogant and aloof.

Consider these references to authority in Timothy Wirth's speech. Again, his topic was global conditions, and his audience was the Washington Press Club and several thousand members of the American public watching the speech on television. Referring to the danger of the increasing use of natural resources, Wirth said: "Professor Tad Homer-Dixon of the University of Toronto warns that in the coming decades, quote, 'resource scarcities will probably occur with a speed, complexity, and magnitude unprecedented in history.'" Wirth went on, "Current conflicts offer a grim foreshadowing of Robert Kaplan's coming anarchy, the anarchy that could engulf more and more nations if we fail to act."[4] Rather than supporting his case, these obscure references to Homer-Dixon and Kaplan damaged Wirth's credibility. Not only did he verbally stumble over the references, but chances are also very good that most of the audience had not heard of at least one of his authorities. How could he have made these references more authoritative and authentic?

First, by ensuring his own familiarity with the authorities, and second, by explaining their credentials to the audience—for example: *"Professor Tad Homer-Dixon of the University of Toronto is one of the world's authorities on environmental security. He has written several widely read articles on how environmental problems can lead to conflict in developing countries and was a keynote speaker at the United Nations conference on population and development in Cairo. Professor Dixon says, and I quote, 'Resource scarcities will probably occur with a speed, complexity, and magnitude unprecedented in history.'"*

Wirth could have augmented his reference to Kaplan as well: *"Current conflicts offer a grim foreshadowing of a coming anarchy that could engulf more and more nations if we fail to act, an anarchy foretold by Robert Kaplan in a frightening recent cover article in the* Atlantic Monthly. *"*By expanding these references, Wirth would have strengthened his own credentials and would have shown more respect for his audience.

EXPERTS WHO ARE "REAL"

It is possible to deepen the connection with the audience even further by telling about your relationship with the expert. Did you read the works of Bertrand Russell as a teenager growing up in the Bronx? Did your father talk to you about life on fall evenings on the porch in San Diego? Did you read every speech that John F. Kennedy ever delivered? Did you study Zen koans at a temple in Kyoto? Explaining the source of your respect for the authority deepens the level of intimacy with the audience, enhancing your credibility and your humanity.

Many of the greatest lessons I have learned have come from people who are close to me and who have gained their expertise through experience. When I quote these people, I am also sharing a part of my life with my listeners, and they sense the authenticity in that sharing. For example, I know a woman minister who began attending seminary in her late thirties. She had been successful in business for the previous fifteen years but had been unhappy with what she perceived as a constant moral dilemma. The decision to give up her career was not easy. She asked everyone she trusted for advice, prayed about her decision every day, and even sought professional counseling on the issue but could not gather the courage to make a decision. Finally, at an evening meeting at the church, she announced that despite a severe shortage of resources and not having a place to live, she was going to leave her job and enroll at a seminary for the fall term.

A month later, this woman was back at the church for the same group meeting, only by then she had secured a scholarship and a place in the student housing center. All of the resources she needed had become available as soon as she had made her decision. That second night she told us, "I always thought that I needed clarity to create commitment, but now

I realize that it is the other way around—it is commitment that creates clarity!"

I use this story as evidence whenever I speak about the power of commitment. It never fails to connect me with my audience and to add a great deal of authority to my remarks. The quotation is not merely an abstraction that I read in some book. The power of the quotation is both in the words, which may be seen as universally true, and in the obvious impact on me, the speaker. The audience appreciates the intimacy inherent in quoting someone I know personally. I was there, the woman was real to me, and that reality gets transmitted to the audience.

An authentic speaker collects the writings and sayings of people who have actually had an impact on her life—not the most popular people or even the most noted authorities (although such people can of course be included). When she quotes those authorities, she also includes the circumstances of her discovering the citation. Such authenticity adds immeasurably to the power of the supplemental authority.

Examples as Evidence

Examples translate abstract proof into experience. They offer the speaker and the audience a story that sparks their sense of reality. Both speaker and listener perceive that the data actually have application in the real world. This realization affects both the delivery of the speaker and the response of the audience.

Jean L. Farinelli, CEO of Creamer Dickson Basford, spoke to a conference of women in business in New Jersey in 1994.

She was imploring her listeners to try going into business for themselves. At one point, she addressed the barriers of founding a new enterprise: "So what about external barriers? Here's an example. Many years ago, an entrepreneur had a very big dream. He needed capital. He went to 301 banks, and 301 banks said 'no' to his dream. Then the 302nd bank said, 'OK, we'll help you build your theme park, Mr. Disney.'"[5]

She went on to use an example even closer to the circumstances of her audience:

> Recently, I talked with Sandie Tillotson, co-founder of Nu Skin International, the skin care products company that grew from nothing in 1984 to $500 million in annual sales today. I asked Sandie about barriers. Her story is inspiring. Picture this: Sandie lives in Utah. In Utah, 98 percent of women are at home. Only two percent are career women—not exactly the best environment for businesswomen role models. Sandie was a teacher when she co-founded Nu Skin in Provo. Almost everyone around her said it was a dumb idea. Sandie calls these people "dream stealers," or people who say your dreams cannot come true. Some do it out of envy, of course, but many do it in a misguided effort to protect women like Sandie from disappointment.[6]

Finally, Farinelli used an example from her own life:

> Let's consider the first subsidiary question: "Can I contribute value to the organization in ways that are not in my job description?" In 1972, I joined Carl Byoir and Associates. At that time, Byoir was the second-largest public relations firm in the world. Most of the role models above me were men. Only one vice president was a

woman. Moreover, I noticed that the men did not line up at my office door, taking bakery numbers, for the chance to become my mentor.

So I used guerrilla tactics. Every time I went to lunch, I sat next to a different vice president. I asked each VP how he succeeded, or, in Byoir terms, how they all got to the eighth floor. After a few weeks of lunches, a pattern emerged. I had broken the code. To get to the eighth floor, you managed a large account. Then you had enough work to spread around the firm, helping many of your colleagues fill up their time sheets.

[. . . In one year,] I had grown my account to $135,000 . . . [and] I began to share the time-sheet wealth. Soon, people on the eighth floor started asking, "Who's that kid on seven?"[7]

Examples bring the speaker into the everyday realm of the audience and move her one step closer to a connection. When used in concert with statistics, examples add immensely to the conviction of the audience. This last account is a personal example, one that Farinelli lived through, feeling the frustrations and elation that go with it. She related this example as a story. The way she related it, the audience will hear it as data, but such examples are near the end of the continuum of evidence for the mind. When the speaker begins to share relevant personal experience, the audience begins to know her as a person rather than merely as a speaker.

Presenting logical support for change is an essential part of leadership speaking. We respect leaders who have the facts in hand, but those who rely only on mental evidence to support their positions are often judged to be uncaring technocrats. Conversely, those who rely solely on emotional appeal and conviction are considered "more real." Both of these judgments are inaccurate. We are all blessed with the ability to reason and the capacity to feel, and it is the integration of these two faculties that is "authentic." The speaker who can communicate both logic and passion is deploying herself fully.

Your audience can make a decision on the basis of logical evidence. But as we have seen, the rate and magnitude of today's change make it difficult to trust the linear predictability of reason. In the next chapter, we will explore ways to appeal to the heart as a way of stirring commitment to your plan for change.

7

WINNING PEOPLE'S HEARTS

Express Your Own Experience and Conviction

▼ Listening to objective evidence, your audience will make at least a tentative decision about the wisdom of making change. But given the illusion of rational certainty, that decision does not guarantee that your listeners will *follow* you— that they will feel real ownership of and commitment to the task. That level of dedication requires trust, something that the strategic mind cannot provide. Accordingly, we turn again to ways of reaching the heart of the audience.

Most of us have had the experience of trusting a leader, believing what he tells us, relying on his integrity as we take action to make his vision of the future come true. We take such action even though he does not always get the details right. We are willing to act, relying on his trustworthiness, believing that he is leading us to change based on our best interest. As we get to know more about the leader, we sense greater commonality with him. We believe that he experiences life as we do, even though he might operate in a different social setting and economic environment. Our faith in him doesn't come from rhetoric; it comes from this experience of connectedness to real life.

It is that need for connectedness that is dominant in today's audiences. Anyone who doubts the informed public's hunger for deeper trust need only note the millions of books sold in recent years by such archetypal psychologists as Thomas Moore, James Hillman, and Jean Shiboda Bolen that promote greater understanding and acceptance of these needs.

The authentic speaker recognizes this commonality as something that will be felt not in the abstraction of an experience but in the experience itself. As a leader invites engagement beyond argument, the audience's confidence in his knowledge will begin to join with trust in his humanity.

Up to now, we have suggested the introduction of credentials and personal qualities, the expression of gratitude, an awareness of resistance, the reflection on shared context, and the presentation of objective evidence as tools to access and express authenticity. In using these tools, a speaker uses primarily the *denotative* capacity of language—its power to describe. In this strictly linear function of language, words are one step removed from reality; they are only an *account* of something that someone did or wants to do.

"One is doomed to remain inarticulate about anything which one hasn't, by an act of the imagination, made one's own."[1] James Baldwin described this process of moving into concert with another—through an act of the imagination. This is the energy available in speaking that is beyond the words themselves, a power actually to evoke a common experience in the speaker and the audience. The tools for such connection are personal experiences, analogies, and metaphors that create images for the audience. When reflecting and writing, including these elements will further enhance your ability to be authentic and to command the trust of your audience when you are speaking.

Personal Experience

Speakers often use stories of heroes to inspire audiences. Each era and culture has its favorites, but athletes and their achievements are standard fare in the modern Western world. Roger Bannister's first sub-four-minute mile provided grist for years of inspiring speeches. The space programs of the former Soviet Union and the United States have also provided stories of heroism to launch new sales programs or inspire marketing representatives to "conquer new frontiers" of sales or productivity. Abraham Lincoln, Winston Churchill, and Thomas Jefferson are the favorites of politicians, and their words and deeds are recalled to inspire new political action. These are all effective to some degree.

But the evidence that transcends the mind and touches the deepest part of the audience is not the recollection of a third party's words or deeds. An audience will not follow a leader because he knows about Roger Bannister or Neil Armstrong. A leader will inspire commitment because the audience is attuned to the personal experience of the leader himself—not the facts of an experience or the circumstances of the experience but the *heart* of the experience, complete with details, feelings, and conclusions.

It is in the personal story that the speaker reveals himself fully, acknowledging his commonality with his listeners not in the things they do or the concepts they believe but in the experiences of life that they live. It is in personal experience that the leader becomes a person, and in sharing that experience, he makes himself accessible to his listeners and therefore worthy of trust, providing a real, attainable, living model for his audience.

In Chapter Two, we focused on the few core ideas that move you to speak and act, and we stressed the fact that these few foundation beliefs are anchored in experience. To the leader, these topics are fundamental themes, and each day, the circumstances of life present opportunities for these themes to play out. Such circumstances can be revealed to the audience as relevant stories—real applications of the principle that the leader seeks to implement. More than facts, more than examples, more than quotations of support, life experience carries with it unshakable authority and undeniable authenticity.

Audiences recognize the significance of these personal revelations on the part of a speaker. During these moments, the speech is transformed into storytelling, a teaching dialogue, where judgment is suspended. Storytelling supports people to find connection in new ways, through emotion, spiritual experience, and intuition. It supports trust in the integrity of the speaker, whether or not the listener believes in the specifics of the proposal.

I can illustrate from my own experience as a speaker. One of my own fundamental values is the freedom and ability to express oneself fully. I'm passionate about this subject, probably as a result of being the smallest kid in my school classes, feeling that I had to speak louder than other kids to be heard. I was also raised on a farm where each member of the family subrogated personal will for the good of the family enterprise. As a final influence, I have an older brother who is substantially larger than I am and who was occasionally willing to use his size to make sure that his little brother didn't become a pest. We have always been close, and are even more so now, but his early influence contributed to my later need to be heard. In short, few circumstances of my early life encouraged me to speak. Therein lies the source of my passion for self-expression. Accordingly, throughout my corporate and teaching career, I've been an excellent proponent of building skills for developing other people—or, in today's jargon, "empowerment."

As a result of this passion for self-expression, I have done some analysis of the components of good delegation. Although most authorities on this subject correctly identify the objective components of delegation—teaching, giving authority, and assigning responsibility—few have acknowledged the subjective or emotional components of delegation. Clearly, when real delegation occurs, the "boss" feels a sense of insecurity, some anxiety that the job will not get done properly. He also feels some loss, as he is letting go of the student, no longer connected by the tether of the teaching relationship.

In speaking on this subject, I advocate the use of subjective measurements to confirm that a manager has truly empowered someone else. I maintain that if you have taught someone well and turned over complete authority and responsibility, you will feel some anxiety and loss. I offer evidence to back this assertion but also use a personal experience to connect with the authentic experience of the audience. My most profound application of delegation has been as a parent. Because everyone in my audience has been a child, and many are currently parents, everyone relates easily to this narrative:

In 1982, I became a single parent and had sole custody and responsibility for my two sons, then thirteen and eleven years old. For the next few years, we grew uncommonly close through a series of personal trials. I had left my career at IBM, and finances had been particularly tight; then I had remarried too hurriedly and had caused some further anxiety. Nonetheless, my children had done well in school and in life, having formed fast friendships and developed solid values. I took tremendous pride (and still do) in their attitude toward life and in the way they conduct themselves.

My older son, Jeff, was admitted to the University of California at San Diego in the fall of 1986, and I elected to drive him to school from San Francisco, a distance of approximately five hundred miles. It was September, but still hot in California's Central Valley along Interstate 5. We drove the ten hours making small talk and generally cracking nervous jokes. I tried to be serious about the future a couple of times but found Jeff only interested in the next months of testing his ability to fend for himself, a very natural concern.

We arrived at the campus in midafternoon, and I helped Jeff move into his dorm room, in the oldest housing on campus but in a choice location and setting. There was a large square carpet of grass in a quadrangle perimetered by six two-story green buildings. On this particular day, it was sparkling with the nervous laughter of new students and the brilliant colors of Southern California clothes.

I helped him move his stuff into his second-story room and started playing "Mr. Mom." I hung pictures, made his bed, and unpacked his Eagle Scout mug. In my concentration, I had failed to notice the growing contingent of kids in the hall, the escalating sound of music, and the lack of interest on his part in what I was doing. To his credit, he was very patient, but when his roommate arrived and they began to compare histories, I realized that I had overstayed. We agreed that I would return that evening to take him to dinner, and I went back to the hotel for a swim. I was beginning to feel anxious.

That evening, just at sunset, I made my way back across the quad to Jeff's room. As I approached, I could see the lights of his room and hear the music of the growing gathering of excited newcomers. By now the group was coed and some people were dancing in the common area. It was difficult to get his attention as I stood at his room door and looked inside.

Everything I had done was changed. The beds were on opposite sides of the room, the pictures had been replaced with posters, and the scout mug was nowhere to be seen. Jeff was engaged in conversation with a group of three students and clearly not pining away for an early dinner with Dad.

Finally, I waved an arm, and he joined me in the hall. I suggested that rather than go to dinner, he should stay with his friends and that I would see him in the morning for breakfast before my drive back up the coast. He protested just enough, then agreed, letting me know that he was looking forward to breakfast.

I hurried down the stairs and into a nearby grove of eucalyptus trees, where I walked alone and cried for about an hour and a half.

This was true delegation. I had done my best to train this young man for the tasks ahead. I now had to give up any pretense of control over his life and let him live it. My role would be only to respond, not to direct. And because I loved him, it hurt.

I've related this experience to audiences many times. It never fails to connect me to my own conviction on the subject, and it rarely fails to connect me with an audience. The feelings that these events engender give me not only a strong advocacy but also a convincing realization that true delegation is difficult, that in the absence of a certain amount of rich and wonderful emotional pain, delegation probably does not happen. Accordingly, I can speak on this subject with a great deal of intensity.

Yet taking Jeff to college was only one experience. My parents' values, my upbringing, my parents' deaths, my experience on the farm, my successes and failures as athlete and scholar, my choice of college, my studies, playing music, my children's births, my career at IBM, running across the United States, trips to the old Soviet Union, the times when I have been hurt, elated, sick, married, divorced—these and all of the other less notable experiences of my life have formed the convictions that compel me to speak. Fortunately, my biography is not yet complete. Experiences that I have today will help form the basis for my conviction in years to come.

So it is with you. Using the relevant experiences of your life to support your advocacy for change is the most effective way of ensuring an authentic bond with an audience.

The Rules of Engagement

As powerful as personal experience is, it is also subject to powerful abuse. Unfortunately, the potential for exploitation is in the attitude of the speaker, not the content of the speech. Nothing taxes a speaker more than trying to memorize a part of his life so that it can be related "sincerely." To a body of listeners, nothing is so clearly manipulative as an attempt to move them with a disingenuous story. Some guidelines can help you avoid these pitfalls.

First, the experience must be clearly relevant to the point you are making in the speech. My colleague Harvey Stone likes to refer to the sharing of irrelevant stories as "therapy," and it certainly has that flavor. If the experience you relate does not support your advocacy, your audience's response will be a resounding "Huh?"

Second, such experiences must be related from memory, not from a script. When I begin the story of taking Jeff to college, I transport myself through imagination back to the car, back to the Central Valley of California. With my son in the passenger seat, I relate what I see and feel during that reverie. I know that my notes only *describe* the actual experience, that the images in my memory will generate a legitimate emotional response, and that the audience will respond in a much more holistic way to that actual memory than to a recitation. Consider this: would someone you trust read you a report of a real incident or relate the actual experience of that incident?

At the 1992 Democratic convention, vice presidential candidate Albert Gore Jr. told the story of his young son's tragic accident in which the child was struck by a car and critically injured. During Gore's speech, at precisely the right time, the television cameras cut to the son, now healthy and waving to the crowd from the candidate's box. Gore read the story from the TelePrompTer, and the child received a thunderous ovation.

When Gore's son was first injured, the senator was often interviewed about the impact of the incident on his life and his political career. His answers were always spontaneous, authentic, and touching. The incident was clearly a turning point in his maturity as a human being. Unfortunately, the version at the convention was cued and rehearsed, and to anyone who had heard the story authentically, its staging at the convention felt like a planned emotional appeal for support. The calculated personal tone, aimed at manipulating rather than connecting, undermined Gore's human credentials. Had he simply ignored the script and read from his internal memory of the day of the accident, letting the camera operators fend for themselves, he might well have connected with himself again and therefore with the audience as well.

The third rule of engagement is to leave nothing out. The memory of a substantive experience includes all aspects of the original happening, the rich sensory details that guide the imagination of the audience and bring your own passion to the surface. Exactly what you saw and heard, exactly what you perceived and felt—these minutiae will turn the experience into one that taps your own heart and the collective heart of the audience.

Finally, you must relate the experience in the first person. When you revert to *you, they,* or *one,* your message becomes an opinion rather than a reality, an example rather than an experience. Listeners may receive the lesson, but they will miss the connection that is so vital to hearing your authentic voice.

Analogy: A Virtual Connection to the Future

Personal analogies show the audience the human face of organizational issues. The story of dropping my son at college is true, and it is directly relevant to the issues of delegation and empowerment. Many listeners have had comparable experiences. The deeper connection comes from the shared values that are obvious but not explicit in the analogy, values that can now be imagined at work. The personal analogy is full of feelings and free of data, and it does not rely on objective evidence to be judged as true. It is live testimony to the possibilities of bringing humanity to the workplace.

CONNECTING THE KNOWN TO THE UNKNOWN

Personal analogies can demonstrate shared values, but *all* analogies can establish a new basis of understanding with the audience. The analogy moves the audience from the known to the unknown by implication. Is the building of the information highway in the 1990s like the building of the automotive highway system in the 1950s? Is cutting corporate cost to avoid layoffs like cutting family costs to avoid bringing college students home from school? Is creating a national health care system analogous to creating the Social Security system? The answers to these questions will bring an audience to a realization of the unknown from a reminder of the known.

CLEAR AND POINTED CONCLUSIONS

The implication of analogy is that the unknown future will be essentially the same as the known past. Accordingly, you must carefully think through any analogy before using it. The audience will make a *complete* association, and some of the conclusions might be counterproductive to your cause. Food biotechnology experts have drawn analogies between the development of genetically engineered food and the development of the monoclonal antibodies used in modern medicine. Though the process is similar, few people want to consider food and medicine as equivalent. One executive even commented, "Within the next few years, you will be able to open your refrigerator and your medicine cabinet and see the same thing!" This image was not helpful to the speaker's cause.

Effective analogies point the audience inexorably toward a conclusion that is in keeping with the speaker's intent. In 1992, Daniel Goldin of the National Aeronautics and Space Administration addressed the Association of Space Explorers in Washington, D.C., on the question of why the United States should send a human expedition to Mars. In setting the stage for his advocacy, he drew the following analogy from the time of Columbus's voyage:

> Only [Queen] Isabella was willing to look beyond the many problems on her own shores and see the potential reward for her investment in the future. The voyages of Columbus set the stage for more Spanish explorers, who

turned Spain into a great world power. As a consequence, the language and culture of Spain prevail in most of Latin America to this day.

On the other side of the world, however, in China . . . the intended destination of Columbus . . . their emperors turned their back on the rest of the world. Sixty years prior to 1492, Chinese explorers had traveled as far as Africa. But a new emperor considered such journeys wasteful extravagances. His successors burned the boats, and banned all Chinese from leaving the country. Those who tried could be executed.

That fifteenth-century decision *not* to explore still reverberates in China today. What was one of the world's most advanced and innovative civilizations is today an inward-looking nation. For a country with the most people on Earth, it is almost an afterthought in global affairs.[2]

This is an apt analogy because the conclusions are unmistakable. The nation that has the foresight to explore space will lead progress in other areas as well. If we fail to fund a mission to Mars, someone else will, and our nation will be forever catching up to other nations with more courage and foresight.

Metaphor: Transferring Characteristics

Whereas analogies lead to a conclusion based on a comparison, metaphors create a picture that can be generalized in the imagination. All of the attributes of the metaphor are ascribed to the new situation, and conclusions are drawn from that image about how entire systems should behave.

In Chapter One, we discussed the changing dominant metaphor for human resources since the 1940s. If human beings are parts of a machine, they will be seen as discreet entities, will be replaced or repaired when they break down, will be the concern of the "maintenance manager," and will become obsolete when more modern parts become available. If these same human beings are "parts of an organism," they will be seen as integral to the whole, will be considered irreplaceable, will be the concern of every other part of the organism, and will receive preventive care. Because a strong metaphor can determine the mind-set for thinking about an entire system, it can be very powerful indeed.

In July 1984, Mario Cuomo introduced the metaphor of the wagon train at the Democratic party's national convention. By tying American progress to this metaphor, he gave voters a choice between survival of the fit and community responsibility.

> The Republicans believe that the wagon train will not make it to the frontier unless some of our old, some of our young, some of our weak are left behind by the side of the trail. The strong, the strong, they tell us, will inherit the land. We Democrats believe . . . that we can make it all the way with the whole family intact. We have. More than once. Ever since Franklin Roosevelt lifted himself from his wheelchair to lift this nation from its knees, wagon train after wagon train to new frontiers of education, housing, peace. The whole family aboard . . . Constantly reaching out to extend and enlarge that family . . . Lifting them up into the wagon on the way . . . blacks and Hispanics, people of every ethnic group, and Native Americans—all those struggling to build their families and claim some small share of America. For

nearly fifty years, we carried them all to new levels of comfort, security, dignity, even affluence.[3]

Most Americans relate well to the frontier of the West; many have ancestors who expanded that frontier, and all can relate to the excitement of unexplored territory. This metaphor worked well, even though Cuomo's candidate was not elected. Any American who saw our political future as a community wagon train voted Democratic. The competing metaphor was a gold rush of rugged individuals, equally effective and a decided victor.

Timothy Wirth called on a metaphor familiar to his audience in his speech on global conditions: "Stated in the jargon of the business world, the economy is a wholly owned subsidiary of the environment. All economic activity is dependent on the environment and its underlying resource base. When the environment is finally forced to file for bankruptcy under Chapter 11 because its resource base has been polluted, degraded, dissipated, and irretrievably compromised, then the economy goes down to bankruptcy with it."[4]

Again, the implications are clear: if we don't take care of the environment, the economy will eventually fail. The metaphor is consistent, and the conclusions are well illustrated.

SUCCINCT METAPHORS

Metaphors needn't be elaborate to be effective. Organized crime, budget deficits, and runaway costs are often referred to as "infectious diseases" or "cancers." These are both powerful metaphors, used frequently to emphasize progressive decay and death. Change is often referred to as "the tide" or "the wind," indicating a force that is beyond listeners' control but within their power to use for their own purposes. The audience fills in the attributes of the metaphor and assigns them to the subject of discussion without further elaboration by the speaker. Metaphors of few words create concrete images and make the abstract take form in the real world.

Richard Mahoney, chairman and CEO of Monsanto, spoke about innovation to the Council on Foreign Relations in 1993 with these images: "Our freedom to innovate is being starved by tax and investment policies that eat our seed corn . . . rather than save it for planting."[5] This has substantially more impact that the abstract translation of the facts: *"Our freedom to innovate is being thwarted by policies that consume our investment capital."*

"Technology is neither the fifth horseman of the apocalypse nor a master to be worshiped. It is a tool we use to create jobs."[6] Again, the abstraction is that *"technology will neither save the world nor destroy it."*

By using the images of the fifth horseman and the master, Mahoney makes the point come to life in the imagination of the listener.

And again, from Tim Wirth: "This depletion [of the water supply in China] is prompting an exodus from the impoverished interior to the booming coastal cities, which along with the demands of rapid industrialization will combine to form an environmental wall that the Chinese economy will soon hit full-speed." There is hardly a need to explain. Wirth is telling us that the Chinese economic train will be destroyed, everyone on board will be killed, and a recovery will not be made for years—very effective.

THE MASTER OF IMAGE

The Reverend Martin Luther King Jr. spun metaphors like webs connecting an intricate and fragile framework of ideas. He would not allow his audiences to wander off into the forest of abstraction when he believed that the work was to be done on concrete city streets. Accordingly, his speeches consistently beseeched his listeners to "see" and remember his words. Some of his metaphors have been memorized by a new generation of activists:

> This is no time to engage in the luxury of cooling off or to take the tranquilizing drug of gradualism.

> No, we will not be satisfied until justice rolls down like water and righteousness like a mighty stream.

> I have a dream . . . that the sons of former slaves and the sons of former slave owners will be able to sit down together at the table of brotherhood; . . . that one day, even the state of Mississippi, a state sweltering with the heat of injustice, sweltering with the heat of oppression, will be transformed into an oasis of freedom and justice.

> With this faith, . . . we will be able to hew out of the mountain of despair a stone of hope; . . . with this faith, we will be able to transform the tangling discords of our nation into a beautiful symphony of brotherhood.[7]

Granted, these images are dramatic and are designed to inspire large groups of people about a continuing issue. But metaphors are used effectively anytime change is discussed, anytime the leader wishes to ascribe the characteristics of a concrete and known image to the concepts being examined.

William Blake's words—"To see a world in a grain of sand . . . / And eternity in an hour"[8]—accurately describe the perspective of this effective leader. The issues of value and meaning that appear in our "personal" lives can indeed be universalized. The leader knows that the longings and the values of people do not change with the area of application. People long to be committed at work and to express their values in their community. Unfortunately, many feel constrained to do so, afraid of the penalty of being incorrect or convinced that their sincerity will be met with the stiff resistance of a bureaucracy. A skilled leader communicates that with regard to values and meaning, every situation can be seen as analogous to all others. A leader who has mastered a metaphorical view of the world can relate his principles with images, instilling a sense of possibility in the imagination of his listeners.

So in the middle of the speech, the leader states the case for the mind and engages the heart. By establishing shared meaning with the audience through context and by focusing the minds of the audience with factual evidence, he creates willing listeners. Then, with personal experience, analogies, and metaphors, he penetrates the tough skin of cynicism and enters a vein of new possibility. Through his own sensitivity, he directs the imagination of his listeners and creates a link with them—not as a military general but as a partner who is privileged to lead, a visionary granted the mantle of guide. Both he and his audience have been persuaded and moved. The listeners now wait for him to ask them to act.

PART FOUR

———

IN CONCLUSION

Endings That Create Beginnings

▼ Thirty to forty minutes have gone by, and the audience has become increasingly interested in what you have to say. If you have been successful in giving meaningful evidence and in tapping your own excitement and conviction, most members of the audience are listening, whether they agree with you or not, whether they fear making the change or look forward to it. The audience has become involved through your directness and authenticity.

Because of this energy, you are the closest to the audience as you near the end of the speech. From this point until you disengage, you will have opportunities to reinforce supporters and diffuse opponents at close range. You can touch them and encounter them intimately, and they can likewise affect you, both as a human being and as a professional. Like a martial artist, you will need to be closely attentive, maintaining your own will and your respect for the audience. Results will flow from your ability to stay in the present and respond honestly.

The members of the audience expect you to invite their involvement in change. Their choices are to refuse your invitation, to act in compliance, or to commit themselves fully to the new direction. To deal effectively with the anxiety of choice requires a clear conclusion, an individually directed request for action, and, in most cases, a period of questions and answers.

The beginning and middle of the speech only prepare the audience to reach the same conclusion as the speaker and to act on that judgment. The impact of the speech can be intensified or diffused by your willingness and ability to maintain your conviction and authenticity in the last few minutes.

8

WRAPPING IT UP

Restate the Choice and Ask for Action

▼ We spoke in Chapter Five about the effectiveness of "sound bites." Short summary sentences can be like advertising slogans, bringing back the associated images without the need to restate the background. The conclusion of the speech works in this very way. A short recapitulation includes some of the same words and images that were used as evidence. These reminders act like a computer macroinstruction, reprompting the mental conviction and emotional experience of the audience with a single brief mention.

A second purpose of the conclusion is to restate the choice that was offered in the beginning of the speech. Now, however, the choice should seem clearer to the audience, as it can be seen against the backdrop of the evidence and experience that the speaker has advanced in the middle of the speech. The conclusion should present, in a succinct narrative, justification and emotional support for the call to action that will follow.

Some of the speeches we have analyzed earlier have included effective conclusions. In the middle of his Notre Dame speech on abortion, Mario Cuomo declared that he could not condone the termination of pregnancy. But he implored the faculty to live their convictions as Catholics, to encourage others to do so, to put their energy into action that would discourage abortion, encouraging mothers to carry babies to term and then taking care of both mother and baby as needed.

However, he also argued through fact and experience that working to change the law, either through constitutional amendment or legislation, was not the right use of energy for the church, for the church needed to live in the secular society as well, to be responsible as a citizen of the democracy that had decided through due process that abortion was a matter of choice for the mother. He concluded:

> The Catholic church has come of age in America. The ghetto walls are gone, our religion no longer a badge of irredeemable foreignness. This newfound status is both an opportunity and a temptation. If we choose, we can give in to the temptation to become more and more assimilated into the larger, blander culture, abandoning the practice of the specific values that made us different, worshiping whatever gods the marketplace has to sell while we seek to rationalize our own laxity by urging the political system to legislate on others a morality we no longer practice ourselves.
>
> Or we can remember where we come from, the journey of two millennia, clinging to our personal faith, to its insistence on constancy and service and on hope. We can live and practice the morality Christ gave us, maintaining his truth in this world, struggling to embody his

love, practicing it especially where that love is most
needed, among the poor and the weak and the dispos-
sessed. Not just by trying to make laws for others to live
by, but by living the laws already written for us by God,
in our hearts and our minds.[1]

In the first sentence, Cuomo brought back the history of the
church he had already reviewed in some depth, including
in his summary the image of ghetto walls. In the third sentence, he begins to present the choice, and in the final
paragraph of this conclusion, he once again makes the key
distinction between church and state that formed the foundation for the entire speech.

Anita Roddick, managing director of The Body Shop International, concluded her stand on corporate responsibility to the International Chamber of Commerce in this way:

What I hope I have done during this talk is to humanize
the issue, stand up for the voices of unrepresented people, grass-roots organizations, and the thousands of
workers that are abused in the race for ever cheaper consumer products. I hope I have spoken on behalf of the
citizens of this planet that believe that we are all in the
middle of the greatest suspense story ever told—whether
we will survive as a species. I hope I have convinced you
that there are other trading networks out there that es-
pouse a gentler, kinder way of doing business, where core
values of community, social justice, openness and environmental awareness are flourishing; that businesses can
transform themselves into organizations that have a vital,
driving sense of responsibility to people and to the
planet.[2]

Roddick revisits her purpose in the first two sentences and at the same time reminds her audience of the ideas and images she has presented during the speech. In the last paragraph, she once again makes the choice apparent, calling on values greater than narrow self-interest to keep her pragmatic audience on moral high ground.

David Pottruck, president and CEO of Charles Schwab and Company, concluded his remarks about diversity as follows:

> What I've related to you this morning through facts and real examples of people you know and love is that the only way to find a passion for diversity is to put yourself in a position where you can be [affected by people] who think, look, or act differently from you.
>
> My understanding of this issue comes from two aspects of my experience. First, as a professional, I see the facts of the market and the pool of potential employees moving us inexorably toward achieving more diversity as a pragmatic business goal. But I also see this issue as a person who has been in the minority and as a person who was impaired by a preconception of other groups of people. To move on the business goal is easy. But to cure false perception requires first a suspicion that you might be missing something and then conscious action on your part to develop an appreciation of what you simply can't see. You *have* to act.
>
> The message should be clear. Diversity is reality. Being in favor of it is like being in favor of Minnesota being cold. The only choices we have are to embrace diversity or not, to encourage it or not, to make decisions based on this reality or to operate in isolation from

our customers and the majority of our future team members. Our only choice is whether to enlarge ourselves to understand and appreciate a bigger and richer world.

Pottruck reminds the audience of both the personal examples he has used and the pragmatic numbers that dictate business reality. He goes on to present the choice as difficult but necessary given the extremely high stakes of the decision.

Finally, consider Jean Farinelli's conclusion of her speech on succeeding in business with the right strategy. She includes the points of her speech explicitly, not by veiled reference. She also singles out her strongest example and reminds the audience of it specifically, encouraging them to remember one particular piece of inspiration.

> Can you succeed in business? Absolutely. At any age. At any time. All you need is the right strategy. And you can find your own "right strategy" if you think big, ask yourself the right questions, and answer them honestly. Don't flinch from the truth or from difficult career choices. The rest will come. It will come because there is no one holding you back.
>
> I mentioned Sandie Tillotson and the "dream stealer." Sandie said she wanted to dispel doubt every day of her business life, so ten years ago, she wrote a Shakespeare quotation in the front of her Day-Timer. It has been there ever since, and she looks at it every day. Here it is: "Our doubts are traitors, / And make us lose the good we oft might win / By fearing to attempt" (*Measure for Measure,* act 1, scene 4).
>
> Sandie reminded herself of her dream every day. Most of us need to do that, so we do not lose our bearings in the vortex of daily business.[3]

All of these conclusions revisit the salient points and experiences relayed in the speech and put them in shorthand for the audience, pointing toward the resolution that the speaker believes to be correct. The summary is an "outline after the fact," drawing the audience and the speaker back to the purpose of the speech and the important evidence used to support that purpose. It is delivered just before the speaker asks listeners to take action, which, as you recall, is what your speech is all about.

The New Future and the Call to Action

All of the energy of the speech is now in a box ready to be released into the new future. In this last and obviously important part of the speech, a leader first describes the future as she sees it, articulating its relevance to the audience and suggesting the broad steps that will be needed to accomplish that future. Second, she asks each person in the audience to actually do something. The first is general; the second is very, very specific.

THE NEW FUTURE

Oscar Wilde described the visionary as a dreamer, "one who can find his way by moonlight, and see the dawn before the rest of the world."[4] The leader is the young Parzival, returning from his quest with a boon, but he has now told us that we must follow him, change our ways, and put ourselves at risk in order to enjoy the future as it could be. The leader now needs to describe the dawn to an audience that remains in the dark. What will we see when the obstacles have been overcome? This is a time not to dwell on the hardship of the journey but rather to see the beauty of the destination. Here are the futures described in some of our examples.

Mario Cuomo wasn't about to change the papal dictates of the Catholic church, nor was he advocating changing the law of the United States. Rather, he pointed his audience to a future of active engagement in the substance of both Catholicism and democracy: "We can be fully Catholic, proudly, totally at ease with ourselves, a people in the world, transforming it, a light to this nation. Appealing to the best in our people, not the worst. Persuading, not coercing. Leading people to truth by love. And still, all the while, respecting and enjoying our unique pluralistic democracy. And we can do it even as politicians."[5]

David Pottruck knew that changing attitudes to embrace diversity would be a long process. He ended his summary, "Our only choice is whether to enlarge ourselves to understand and appreciate a bigger and richer world," then continued to describe this world to his audience:

> This new world at Charles Schwab, a world that will be here in the next few years, will hold more opportunity for advancement than we could possibly see today. Our company will double in size, each of you will be challenged to redefine yourself, not by your title in the company, but by your talent in the world. You will be asked to contribute to teams that care for customers from a wide range of backgrounds, who think differently, act differently and make different investment decisions than do customers today. You will be E-mailing messages to Hong Kong, Bangkok, Paris, and Rio de Janeiro; and you will be wondering, in times of reflection, how we got here.

Anita Roddick's vision of the future in which companies are considerate of communities: "If all of us in business committed ourselves to such an attitude and such undertakings, big things would indeed happen. We could keep rural life vital and feasible, rather than watch millions more [people] stream into the squalor of cities that can't grow fast enough to keep up. We could help build political stability and sustainable democracy. We could develop a new image and ideal of business that caused less transitional pain and more transformational economic gain."[6]

These are "visions of the dawn" worth commitment. The first time the leader spoke of them was early in the speech, when telling of the best outcome of change and warning of the worst outcome of not changing. By relating the vision again at the end of the speech, the leader sets the foundation for action on the part of the audience, action that will begin the process of reformation.

A REQUEST FOR ACTION

This is the acid test, the step in a speech for change that is most often skipped, even by the most convincing and passionate speakers. For some reason, many people don't believe that we have the right to ask others to act, even on issues that define us. In my experience, the willingness to ask for action and expect it is an unmistakable attribute of a leader. It is the leader's responsibility to spend the necessary contemplative time searching her experience and reviewing the context to gain conviction about the human value of her proposal. It is her responsibility to do the necessary research to become convinced that the evidence supports her decision. And once her heart and mind are in concert, it is her responsibility to call clearly for action on the part of the people she is charged to lead.

As we said in Chapter Six, a leader can build credibility by building belief in her words. But she can instill committed action only by building trust in herself. At the end of the speech, she must ask for the manifestation of that commitment. It takes confidence to act on your own conviction. It takes real courage to ask another human being to do so. Robert Terry concludes in his meticulous study *Authentic Leadership: Courage in Action,* "If there is one dominant connection" in the historic definitions of leadership, "it is action."[7] The leader can observe, contemplate, study, and speak, but change happens only with action.

After seeing and communicating the vision of change, the leader must implement, and she must do so using the inspiration and labor of others. The action can be simple and easy to perform, but it must be definitive.

WHAT CAN I DO NOW?

Frequently, a leader does not consider what action individual members of her audience can actually take and proposes a list of sweeping "reforms" that are far beyond the ability of any single person in the audience to effect. Listeners become convinced that the issue is too large for their involvement; each person believes that "they," not "I," will handle the action. But the nature of commitment is that it is personal, and it requires an act of faith. Asking only for the implementation of a broad-scale and far-reaching agenda redirects the leader's remarks away from the individuals who now share her vision and toward that entity that has no power to commit. She addresses her request to "the company," "the department," or "the state." Leaders do this frequently in the name of seeing the big picture—calling for a list of reforms and leaving listeners with the sense that the problem is just too big for them to act at all. A broad agenda may be appropriate, but if you have delivered well, the audience members really *want* to be part of your vision, *want* to be part of this new and exciting world you have called for. Asking for a simple, definitive action on their part will test the seal of your bargain.

Anita Roddick asked for simple steps to enhance corporate responsibility, but she addressed her call to the International Chamber of Commerce, the *organization,* rather than the people in it, people she had connected with in her earlier remarks. She reverted to an impersonal call:

> I ask that the ICC move now on aggressively expanding its efforts to develop a Corporate Code of Conduct . . . a formal, articulated, and well-defined set of principles which all of its members agree to live up to. A broadly adhered-to Code of Conduct would shut down the excuse about competition making ethical behavior impossible once and for all . . . we could all agree not to compete in ways destructive to communities or the environment. The various commissions and councils of the ICC must not be focused on lobbying for business interests against citizens groups; we should focus more on developing rigorous and broad standards for ourselves.[8]

It was not the *organization,* however, that found poignancy in Roddick's vivid description of holding babies who were deformed by toxic waste. It was not the *organization* that felt pride in her description of the Nanhu women of Mexico who keep their village together by making body scrubs from cactus fiber. No *organization* thinks or feels or listens. Appealing to the organization is the last-ditch avoidance of authenticity, the final escape from the kind of personal leadership needed to engender spirited action. Yet the adjustment is simple, if not easy. I would suggest the following:

> We desperately need a communal Code of Conduct to support our individual values. None of you, and certainly not I, want peoples of the world who are already impoverished to suffer more at our individual hands. It is our organizations that stand in our stead, and it is with our organizations that we can support each other to stop using competition as an excuse for unethical and destructive behavior.
>
> I'm asking each of you who know the truth of what I've described to take one action during this conference to show your support for drawing up a such a code. The representatives of the committee charged with that task are listed in the program, and they are all here and reachable. Make it your individual sign of integrity to see at least one of them during this conference and express your view on this subject.

Would there be squirming in the seats? Probably. But at least some of the delegates would actually do what Roddick asked, and a committed group would be formed through concerted action. The leader can't hope for immediate consensus, but she can ask and expect action from the first wave of converts.

David Pottruck asked each person in Schwab for a modest sign of commitment to valuing diversity: "In the next week, seek out only one person that you know sees the world differently than you do. Find something to talk about, even if it is only this speech. Discuss the pros and cons of our emphasis on diversity—your fears and particularly your hopes about it. If you will do only that much, you will begin to open new possibilities for our company and for yourself."

Just as the statement of purpose defines the speech at the beginning, so the summary, the description of the new future, and the call for action begin the movement toward change. When you lead, you must ask for personal action.

What Is Left?

The very end of a speech is not unlike the very beginning in its import. Just as real gratitude based on specific memories helps establish authenticity at the beginning, it can reinforce authenticity at the end. Is it obvious that "thank you" should be the last message? Yes, it is. Is it a convention of speaking to say "thank you"? Yes, it is. But real gratitude is rarely experienced or delivered. The *words* are said often, but only infrequently does a speaker actually reconnect with the audience in these last moments. Here again, convention presents a great opportunity to make a deep and lasting impression.

I am surprised every time I stop and survey the faces of students after a final lecture at the university or of clients after a speaking program. Invariably, I become aware of how much I have been energized from the interchange and of how much these people have trusted me for insight and inspiration. Students rarely miss the lectures, and they are supportive of classmates in their remarks, their tone, and their demeanor. They actively engage in the subject of leadership and participate fully in speaking from their deepest convictions. I consider this kind of attention a gift. What they owe me, and what they owe themselves, is to be in the seat every week and to do the assignments. Everything else comes from attention. Accordingly, I frequently experience gratefulness, and I usually say so as the class closes for the semester. Usually, it is with words very similar to those in this paragraph.

The same is true of all audiences. Any person who listens to an appeal for change is showing respect for the speaker. If you have been able to generate any engagement with listeners or any real conviction in yourself, you have gone beyond the pale of the ordinary. Followers owe you absolutely nothing until you have earned their commitment with reflection, clarified your thoughts with a discipline like writing, and spoken to them as a real human leader, not as person who holds a position more senior in the hierarchy than their own.

If I were speaking to you now, I would say something like this:

> In closing, I want to assure you that I realize that change is difficult and that what I have called for here is taxing in light of the values of the modern world. I have asked for more time in exchange for more substance. I have asked for more reflection, more precision, and more vulnerability. In most ways, what I have called for is funda-

mentally different from what you may have learned before about speaking to others. Still, you have been patient and engaged.

I take your willingness to read through this book, to listen seriously to my call for change, as a sign of respect for me and for what I have written, an indication of value. We need to change the way we communicate now. And in the weeks and months ahead, you will hear more from me and from others, imploring you to consider the need to engender commitment in the people who ultimately operate our organizations. But for your attention alone, I am grateful. It is a great gift. Thank you very much.

9

ANSWERING QUESTIONS AUTHENTICALLY
Feedback at the "Town Hall"

▼ A conventional book on public speaking would end with the preceding chapter. Yet one of our premises is that the requirements of leadership have changed as the needs of followers and organizations have changed. The effective speech is no longer predominantly a one-way communication; it is an authentic interactive dialogue. Because the leader wants to inspire commitment to change, he needs to pay strict attention to the feedback from listeners, to their *actual* reaction rather than their *expected* reaction, not with the intent of altering his remarks but for the purpose of responding to the audience's concerns. To be authentic is to listen to silent feedback during the speech and to invite explicit feedback after it. The speech isn't over when you have finished your monologue. Really hearing the reaction of the audience is a vital sign of authenticity.

There is feedback in *every* communication. Only by blocking our natural reactions can we avoid showing or noticing the response. A speaker who wants to be heard will know

137

when he is *not* being heard. Some cultures, of course, encourage avoidance of engagement. In the Far East, Western speakers often wonder if they are even understood. In these cultures, formality and detachment dictate the muting of reaction. But in the West, we have little patience with stoicism. Speeches about change generate frowns and smiles, encouragement and disenchantment. A speaker can gauge his effectiveness by noticing these signs of life.

Questions from the audience are the most direct kind of feedback and therefore offer the best chance to engage. In agreeing to respond to questions, you offer a direct relationship with individuals rather than the group as a whole. You build expectations of candor in the audience and can greatly enhance or damage the credibility and trust you have constructed during the speech. Your success will depend on how you respond when the questions—particularly the tough ones—are finally asked.

When to Offer, When to Refrain

Maintaining trust requires that you be willing to answer questions, but it is not always appropriate to take them. The two primary considerations are the content of the speech and the size of the audience. If the speech is your first advocacy for this change, it is likely to be more abstract and less specific, written to inspire with context and values. Questions could prove frustrating for both you and your listeners and could drain away the excitement that has been generated. If the audience is large, taking questions is logistically difficult. The process needs to be tailored both to allow representative questions to be asked and to avoid ill feelings in someone not recognized due to time constraints. If you combine these two negative influences, delivering an abstract, value-based speech to a large audience, you should refrain from offering the audience a chance to ask questions. Imagine Martin Luther King Jr. finishing the "I Have a Dream" speech by asking for questions from the hundred thousand people in front of the Lincoln Memorial. And imagine the questions that might be forthcoming—"Uh, just how often do you have this dream, Dr. King?"

If size of audience and nature of material are not prohibitive, you should always offer the audience the chance to clarify, contribute to, or challenge your comments. The format of the town hall meeting is popular because when audiences can really participate, they are more likely to feel ownership and commitment. If you can conduct the question-and-answer period displaying the same competence and connection that were obvious in your more formal remarks, you can further solidify the trust of the audience.

Being Yourself in Real Time

At the start of this book, we explained the purpose of structuring the speech, of working with a template that would guide you toward finding and speaking with your authentic voice. Structure and discipline can also guide you toward authenticity in the question-and-answer period, but there is a substantial difference between this postlude and the speech itself. The process of composing speeches is one of contemplation, discussion, documentation, reading, revision, and reflection. As you compose, you can explore the history of the issue and look to your human experience for meaning and relevance. You can carefully scrutinize the evidence for truth and consult with others whom you respect. The process gives you every chance to avoid arrogance and defensiveness and to display an attitude of confidence. Writing and revising compel your attention; they challenge the self, exposing the most subtle deception. Composing a speech is a long process of trial and error.

But in the question-and-answer session, all of this must happen in real time. In the short interval between the finish of the question and the beginning of the response, the authentic answer goes through your consciousness very quickly. During questioning, your natural tendency is to defend, patronize, and avoid exposure. It takes a planned process and practice to avoid these tendencies and stay within yourself, speaking in a way that continues to engender trust.

A Template for Answering Authentically

The following guidelines are designed to help you notice the truth as it flashes through your consciousness and to respond to questions authentically and effectively.

RESPONDING TO BOTH QUESTIONS

Each question from the audience is really two questions, the *stated* one, which is literal, and the *unstated* one, which is only hinted at by the words of the question. The first task of the speaker is to discern when these two questions coincide and when they don't. The second task is to respond to both. In doing so, the speaker can indeed display competence and generate a new level of trust. The stated question is the obvious, objective one; the unstated one is the intent of the questioner, revealed in the subtleties of voice, body, and attitude.

CLASSIFYING FOR CLARITY

Each question stands alone and reflects both the background and knowledge of the questioner and the context of the speech itself; but thinking about questions in *categories* can be helpful as you learn to be more discerning. Questions generally fall into three groups: contributions, requests for clarification, and disputes or challenges.

Contributions are not really questions but rather comments of support. The "questioner" wants to be heard as sympathetic (the unstated intent) and elects to elaborate on the positive nature of one of the points of your speech by giving additional evidence or examples. If you agree that the example or experience of the questioner is appropriate, such contributions are easy to handle.

Requests for information and clarification are also easy to respond to. The stated and unstated questions are the same, and negative feelings are generally absent. The questioner merely missed a point or wants some clarification about what you said.

Both contributions and requests can be handled easily by acknowledging the question, commenting or clarifying, and confirming that you have been responsive. These three steps are fundamental in responding to every inquiry.

But most questions asked after a speech advocating change are not contributions or requests. They are *disputes* or *challenges* and are often disguised in the rhetorical clothes of the other categories. This means that the stated and unstated questions are not the same. Such questions call for maximum awareness and skill on the part of the speaker; they are rife with both opportunity and risk.

ANSWERING AUTHENTICALLY

Defensiveness will erode trust. If you can find agreement with the questioner and respond to both the intent of the question and the feelings of the questioner, you can continue to earn the faith of your audience.

At a recent conference on illegal drug use in New York, the primary speaker advocated spending more federal money on drug treatment services. She entertained a "question" from a listener who immediately agreed with the speaker's context and went on to suggest the abolition of the federal drug enforcement effort. The questioner finished with an endorsement of drug legalization.

The instinctive response would have been to defend against the subtle attack: *"I don't believe that legalization is an answer to the drug problem. I think it is shortsighted, sends the wrong signal to the wrong population at the wrong time, and would kill far more of our young people than the current rash of drug violence."*

This answer is, of course, technically correct from the speaker's point of view, but it is responsive only to the disagreement with the questioner. Had the speaker confirmed common ground with the questioner (the context of the problem), acknowledged the feelings that were present (frustration and anger), and then made the distinction in their positions (legalization versus treatment), she could actually have maintained mutual respect and reinforced her own solution—for example:

> I appreciate your support for an increase in our investment in treatment. But I also hear your deep dissatisfaction with the drug enforcement effort and our level of federal spending to support that activity. Your comments reflect the frustration of many who see drug crime continue to rise with an ever-increasing death toll among our young. I share that frustration.
>
> While we seem to agree that increased treatment will have an impact on those already addicted, I believe it would be bad policy to signal our youth that illicit drugs in *any* quantity would be appropriate to use. I believe, in fact, that the enforcement effort over the years has been a holding action, effective at maintaining pressure on supply while we have been developing our understanding of demand reduction strategies. The next few years of a more balanced approach of supply and demand reduction should yield even better results.

This response emphasizes the area of agreement, acknowledges the feelings of the questioner, and still makes the distinction in the two positions. The key elements are speaking to the common ground and openly acknowledging the intensity and opinion of the questioner. Like openly acknowledging resistance in the beginning of a speech, these aspects of the "answer" can deepen the connection between speaker and questioner and can signal a level of safety to the rest of the audience.

Disputes can also be disguised as simple requests for clarification. For example, slight differences in wording or tone can signal differences in intent. "I was having trouble hearing you from the back of the room. I believe you said that the company would save four million dollars in the first year of this change. Is that the correct number?" Clearly, this is a request for clarification. But "I believe you said that the company would save four million dollars in the first year of this change, but *I couldn't believe my ears—is that the correct number?*" is something more.

Similarly, "How many people will relocate to Detroit to accomplish the transfer of work?" is a request for more information, but "How many people will *have to move* to Detroit to accomplish the transfer of work?" might convey disenchantment with the request.

Just such delicacies of wording can signal differences in the intent of the question. And not all questions are so obvious; some questioners hide their intent even more effectively. They could ask the question with the right words but a voice full of cynicism. They might ask while seated with arms folded defiantly. Such body language signals are available to all speakers.

Unfortunately, convention allows a speaker to ignore or evade the unpleasant. Dealing with anger, disappointment, or disagreement is uncomfortable. The temptation is strong to treat these questions as though the intent is stated in the words, and of course, you will rarely be criticized for ignoring indirect challenges. The questioner hides the intent to avoid direct confrontation, and the speaker detects the veil but ignores it to avoid dealing with the real issue of the questioner. This is an insidious conspiracy. Authenticity demands that this bargain not be kept, and the first to acknowledge the real agenda gains the respect and admiration of the entire audience.

Challenges and disputes, whether hidden and subtle or open and aggressive, present opportunities for new levels of engagement with the audience. Both require the same elements to bring the engagement with the questioner to a satisfactory conclusion. These are the complete guidelines:

> Repeat the stated question *and* the unstated one (the intent) so that the audience and the questioner know what you have heard.
> Answer the stated question.
> Find a way to say *yes* to the questioner.
> Acknowledge the feelings behind the dispute or challenge.
> Find and articulate the distinction in the challenge and your own belief.
> Respond to the unstated question.
> Confirm that you have at least been responsive.

This is a long instruction, and like the sequence we've suggested for the speech itself, the steps serve as a map toward an authentic response. Practicing them will make you more thoughtful, less defensive, and more responsive to followers and will also strengthen your authority as a leader.

Let's look at an example. At a town hall meeting of two hundred senior managers in the southwestern United States, the CEO of an American company was entertaining questions. He had spoken earlier about a bright future for the company and had implored attendees to look to both revenue enhancements and cost savings in their respective operations. Because this was a public company, the CEO's seven-digit annual salary and bonus figure had been printed in the paper the previous week. The latest quarter's performance had been good but not fantastic. He is a very popular CEO, well respected in the company.

This question came from a field manager. The tone was flat and noncommittal: "I have an employee who is the backbone of our operation. She comes in early in the morning, stays late at night, takes the initiative to solve customer problems, and is the cheerleader for the rest of the office. Her job classification doesn't qualify her for stock options in our company. Now, you make a lot of money, much more than I do, and I'm sure you deserve it. What are we doing about passing the opportunity for options down to employees like her?"

Attending as a consultant, I was seated in the back of the room, calmly listening to the questions. The CEO, however, was seated on a stool on the stage with bright lights in his eyes, faced with responding in a cogent way while keeping up appearances. The stated question was "Are we going to lower the requirements for employees to qualify for stock options?"—a request for information. The veiled intent was to question the CEO's pay scale. The feelings were resentment and probably some anger, and the real question was a challenge: "Why do you make so much money when the rest of us do all of the work?" At some level of consciousness, everyone in the room heard the real question.

The CEO launched into an answer to the stated question, reviewing the history of the option plan, reminding the audience of the many ways in which employees could gain ownership in the company, and explaining why the option plan was reserved for employees of a certain level. When he was finished, he asked the questioner if he had answered the question. The questioner said, "I guess so," and left it at that. This CEO did exactly what most of us would do, only he did it slightly better.

Later, I reviewed the meeting with him, and when I came to this question, I asked him if he had heard what I had heard. The session had been tape-recorded, so I played the question back from the recording, and he remembered the split second when he had heard everything—the words, the intent, and the feelings. In less time than we can measure, he had chosen his answer because his underlying instinct was to protect, defend, and justify.

We reviewed other possibilities and decided on this one:

> Tom has asked about our reasons for limiting stock options to directors and above, but I hear some other concerns in his question as well, concerns that go to the issue of executive compensation in relationship to the pay of others. In case I'm right about that, I want to respond to those issues as well. *(Repeat the stated question as well as the intent.)*
>
> First, on the issue of options. We have found over time that employees below a certain pay level use options only as additional compensation. They execute their options and cash them in right away. The purpose of any stock ownership plan is to encourage people who work in the company to have a real stake in the company's performance. So we think that the opportunities that we have to purchase stock in 401(k) programs accomplish

that purpose. Above and beyond that, everyone can buy stock at a discount through the stock purchase plan, and there are no restrictions on how long you must hold that stock. Does that respond to that part of your question, Tom? *(Answer the stated question.)*

Now, on the larger issue of executive compensation, I want you to know that I appreciate anyone who cares enough about the company to be concerned about this, and I particularly admire his courage in asking *me* that question. He pointed out that the real heart of this company is employees like the one he described, people like you who come to work in the branches every day and interface directly with our customers. I know and appreciate that, as does every member of the executive team. If we aren't telling you that enough, then we need to get out more.

The whole issue is the subject of much publicity right now, and Tom's question gives me a reason to speak to it directly. I have an interest, as you do, in making sure that our company is spending its compensation dollars in the best possible way. *(Find a way to say yes to the questioner and acknowledge the feelings behind the challenge.)*

As some of you know, executive compensation is set by the board of directors—specifically, by a committee of outside directors. We set it up this way to avoid any appearance of being self-serving and to ensure that we emphasize long-term results rather than short-term movement in the stock price. That means that the officers are paid the bulk of their compensation on the basis of long-term objectives and a smaller portion on year-to-year operations. For a company in our stage of development, that seems like the right course to me. *(Find the distinction in the challenge and your own belief.)*

The compensation committee also ensures that we are competitive in our industry so that the officers don't go over to competitive firms because of our shortsightedness. In all, the process seems correct, but it is certainly open for any of you to inquire about further.

This morning, I talked about the need for all of us to improve our revenue stream and control costs. Those objectives are in keeping with our plan for more long-term investment next year to fuel what we see as dramatic growth. At the end of our five-year plan, I believe we will all see that the investments we are making now in compensation will have been well placed and that they will result in greater opportunity for all of us. *(Respond to the unstated question.)*

I hope that I have clarified the issue, Tom, and again, I appreciate your bringing it up. *(Confirm that you have been responsive.)*

This was obviously easier to compose after that fact, and we did not use it as a "revision" for the questioner. Rather, constructing this "perfect" answer was part of coaching this CEO to respond more authentically the next time he encountered a similar situation.

As we said at the beginning of the chapter, everything that you have had time to digest and consider in the development of the speech itself requires your attention in a split second during the question-and-answer session. Practice and review can provide you with the reminders you need to respond more effectively in the future.

The Last Word

In the town hall format, the clock often has the final say. But to complete your message, after the response to the last question, you need to deliver a final piece of compelling evidence. If you don't, the audience will simply wander off, remembering the answer to the last question rather than the major point of your speech. H. Ross Perot is a master of such focused endings. In 1993, Perot spoke to the National Press Club for thirty-five minutes about the welfare system in the United States, decrying the fiscal and psychological impact of the growth of entitlement programs. A protracted question-and-answer period followed, and after the last question, the time-conscious host tried to wish Perot a quick goodbye. Perot held up his hand for quiet, got it, and reached under the lectern to produce a large framed picture of Chief Seattle, a Native American hero of the early nineteenth century. Everyone in the room was familiar with the negative effect that relocation to reservations and government subsidies have had on the Native American society.

Perot simply said: "I want you all to remember that this is an example of what happens when you deny a person the ability to hunt. The welfare system in the United States is doing just that to an entire generation of Americans. We should stop it."

Without doubt, everyone in the room remembered the point of Perot's speech. This last word is essential for just that purpose. Save one piece of compelling evidence to reinforce your major premise at the very end.

The closing of the engagement is like the beginning in that a good deal of convention surrounds it. Authenticity is not the rule but rather the exception. And mastery of this new set of skills takes constant awareness and frequent practice. Each time you hear and consider a question more consciously, you will get closer to yourself, respond from what you authentically heard, and as a result get closer to the audience. In the question-and-answer period, your heart and mind are called into rapid play, and your human instinct to protect yourself plays the foil. At the end of the speech, consciousness is at a premium, and the opportunity to connect is immense.

EPILOGUE

Passion Inspires Commitment

▼ I've suggested in these pages that the practice of real self-expression is becoming obsolete, and with its demise, trust in our leaders continues to erode. We have become used to judging appearance rather than substance, yet as the world continues to change, our need for grounding in reality becomes greater and our frustration with imitations more profound.

To speak effectively as a leader in this new interdependent world will require a reversal of this trend, a defying of convention that has snared us in fantasy. Leading is about inspiring others to make change, and organizational leaders who foster joint commitment to meaningful endeavor will excel. Those who still depend on engendering passive compliance will falter. It is the energy of collective conviction that will fuel answers to the complex questions of global competition, national social malaise, or international cooperation.

People make commitments to causes they value and to

people they respect and trust. Rediscovering an authentic voice and maintaining a commitment to meaningful change are requisites for any leader who would respond to these needs. Such authenticity requires speaking from both the mind and the heart, directly to the minds and hearts of the audience. When listeners sense both competence and connection, they are willing to engage, consider their own commitment, and eventually act.

Ideas can be learned from others, but passion lives in our own experience. The first step of effective advocacy is to rediscover what is personally meaningful by reflecting on the actual shaping events of our lives. Increasing knowledge of internal truth must be a central theme in the leader's life and will, as a discipline, tend to deepen all of her messages. Perhaps that deepening can slake the technological thirst to make shallow messages more broadly heard. Technology can replace all of the parts of the body, but it cannot synthesize the whisper of the human spirit. By paying attention to our most important urgings, however, we can amplify that whisper to an audible call. Having thus reexperienced our own conviction, we can begin to bring it to others.

From the introduction until the last question is answered, the speech can become a vehicle to carry the audience to decision and commitment. By including both facts and feelings, by exposing both credentials and personal qualities, and by entering into the interaction with the audience honestly and completely, a speaker can offer real meaning in addition to the objective of shared accomplishment.

Because we are out of the practice of being real, I have offered a template or structure that will encourage the use of both objective and subjective evidence and will engage the speaker as well as the audience. But because authenticity depends on your intent, the only guarantee of success will come from your own subscription to these ideas and your dedication to rekindling that intent each time you speak.

I know from experience that consciousness doesn't come easy; it comes in hard-earned billionths of a second. But there are ways of training ourselves to expand those moments to full seconds, minutes, hours, and sometimes days. When we communicate authentically, we add immensely to the possibility for others to do the same and for real leadership to emerge once again in the human family and to defeat cynicism one encounter at a time.

I realize, too, that our world has made authenticity more frightening, even to the most stalwart of souls. There may be a price to pay in terms of ridicule by those who can't match your courage, but that is the price of leadership. Authentic does not mean indecisive; vulnerable does not mean weak; and we need not abandoned the mind to listen to the heart.

It takes work to remember that we are connected first as human beings, rather than only through our roles as professionals, capitalists, politicians, or students. In our lives of planning and executing, the reality of our humanness, and its inseparability from the parts we play, rarely surfaces unless we make time and develop the discipline to see it. This book is meant to encourage you to take that time, to provide a discipline for you to use, and to implore you to convey your discovery to others actively and authentically. The people you lead will be richer and more successful for it, and so will you.

RESOURCE

The Elements of an Effective Authentic Speech

Each element of the speech is composed to bring out the authentic expression of the speaker.

I. Beginning

A. Introduction (pp. 41–47)
Establishes credentials and creates a foundation for trust.
- Include only what is relevant to the subject or important to the audience.
- Include both professional credentials and personal qualities.
- Draft suggested remarks for the introducer.
- Be prepared to supplement the introduction in the first part of the speech.

B. Appreciation (pp. 47–53)
Conveys authentic gratitude, deepens audience connection.
- Be specific. Recount instances that are examples of the source of your appreciation of the audience.
- See list of questions, p. 51.

C. Purpose (pp. 54–57)
Invites conflict and engagement.
- State your purpose clearly and with positive provocation.

D. Acknowledging resistance (pp. 58–62)
Demonstrates empathy, creates an opening to be heard.
- Acknowledge the existence of resistance in your audience.
- Name the feelings of resistance as well as the conflicting opinions.

E. Stating the stakes (pp. 63–66)
Quickly establishes the benefits of change and the consequences of remaining in the status quo.
- State the importance concisely; offer no evidence at this point.
- State the "best case" and the "worst case."

II. Middle

Organized as a story: where we've been, where we are, and where we are going.

A. Context (pp. 71–85)

Sets out the meaning of the change you are advocating.

- Establish a common understanding of the culture.
- Trace the history of the issue to the present.
- Put the issue in the setting of other issues.
- State the common, larger values that the change will reinforce.
- Surround "sound bites" with meaning by including a background statement that frames the declaration.

B. The body of evidence (pp. 85–88)

Presents the arguments for change.

- Be brief and simple.
- See list of questions, pp. 85–86.

C. Evidence for the mind (pp. 89–102)

Satisfies the audience's need for objective proof; justifies a decision from the audience.

- Use specific data, not generalities.
- Explain the impact of the proof on the audience.
- Use familiar examples for illustration.
- State your relationship to any expert you quote.
- Ensure the audience's familiarity with authorities you cite.

D. Reaching the heart (pp. 103–120)

Satisfies the audience's need for connection; assists the audience in making a commitment.

- Use personal experience that is relevant.
- Tell stories from memory, not a script.
- Use sensory detail to tap your own passion.
- Avoid abstractions not supported by your personal experience.
- Create images with analogies and metaphors that are powerful for you and familiar to the audience.

III. End

A. Conclusion (pp. 123–128)

Reminds the audience of the evidence and the feelings of the speech.

- Recap by using some of the same words and images from the speech.
- Restate the choice that was offered in the beginning of the speech.

B. The new future (pp. 128–130)

States your vision of the future in concrete terms.

C. Call to action (pp. 130–134)

Asks each member of the audience to demonstrate commitment through some change in performance.

- Make the call specific and individualized.

D. Closing (pp. 134–136)

Reinforces the audience's belief in your competence and trust in your humanity.

- Find real gratitude for the audience's attention, and express it.

IV. Question-and-Answer Session

Some questions are merely contributions to your point of view or real requests for clarification or more information. These are relatively easy to handle. Most questions, however, contain some element of disagreement or dispute that can be heard by the speaker who is sensitive to the questioner and willing to engage.

A. Answering challenging questions (pp. 137–149)
- Listen for both the stated question and the unstated question.
- Classify the question for clarity.
- Answer authentically:
    Repeat the stated and unstated question.
    Answer the stated question.
    Find a way to say yes to the questioner.
    Acknowledge the feelings.
    Find the distinctions between the challenge and your position.
    Respond to the unstated question.
    Confirm that you have been responsive.

B. Having the last word (pp. 150–151)
Save one powerful piece of evidence that will bring the audience back to the point of your speech after the last question has been answered.

NOTES

Chapter One

1. L. Uchitelle, "The Rise of the Losing Class," *New York Times,* Nov. 20, 1994, sec. 4, p. 1.
2. M. Wheatley, *Leadership and the New Science* (San Francisco: Berrett-Koehler, 1992), p. 150.
3. Ibid., p. 64.
4. M. Kelly, "The Game," *New York Times Magazine,* Oct. 31, 1993, p. 62.
5. M. Parris, "Don't Prompt Me, I'm Speaking," *London Times,* Oct. 6, 1993, p. 14.
6. C. Handy, *The Age of Unreason* (Cambridge, Mass.: HBS Press, 1990), p. 135.
7. V. Havel, "Surviving Together," *ISAR,* Spring 1992, pp. 4–5.
8. T. Melohn, *The New Partnership* (Essex Junction, Vt.: Oliver Wight, 1994), p. 224.

Chapter Two

1. W. Bennis and others, "Learning Some Basic Truisms About Leadership," in M. Ray and A. Rinzler (eds.), *The New Paradigm in Business* (New York: Putnam, 1993), p. 77.
2. W. Bennis, *On Becoming a Leader* (Boston: Addison-Wesley, 1992), p. 122.
3. M. Cuomo, *More than Words: The Speeches of Mario Cuomo* (New York: St. Martin's Press, 1993), pp. xvi, xviii.
4. J. Hillman and M. Ventura, *We've Had a Hundred Years of Psychotherapy—and the World's Getting Worse* (San Francisco: HarperSanFrancisco, 1992), p. 53.
5. M. Cuomo, *More than Words*, p. xvii.
6. R. Commanday, "Repin Flawless in Technique," *San Francisco Chronicle*, Dec. 12, 1992, "Datebook," p. 32.

Chapter Three

1. P. Kugler, *Mirror, Mirror on the Wall*, 1992 (audiocassette).
2. M. Cuomo, *More than Words*, p. 35.
3. R. Mahoney, "China: Still the World's Top Emerging Marketplace," *Vital Speeches of the Day*, 1993, *59*(16): 489.
4. H. R. Clinton, "Health Care: We Can Make a Difference," *Vital Speeches of the Day*, 1993, *59*(19): 580.

Chapter Four

1. G. B. Shaw, *Man and Superman* (New York: Viking Penguin, 1947 [1946]).
2. N. L. Reinsch, "The Mission of a University Is to Create Knowledge," *Vital Speeches of the Day*, 1993, *59*(16): 501.
3. A. Roddick, "Corporate Responsibility," *Vital Speeches of the Day*, 1994, *60*(7): 196.
4. Ibid.

Part Three

1. J. M. Kouzes and B. Z. Posner, *The Leadership Challenge: How to Get Extraordinary Things Done in Organizations* (San Francisco: Jossey-Bass, 1987), p. 113.

Chapter Five

1. S. J. Gould, "The Strike That Was High and Outside," *New York Times,* Nov. 19, 1984, sec. 1, p. 23.
2. R. Rosenberg, "Components of Success," *Vital Speeches of the Day,* 1993, *59*(21): 656.
3. J. Adams, "Juggling Job and Family," *Vital Speeches of the Day,* 1994, *60*(4): 125.
4. P. Senge, *The Fifth Discipline: The Art and Practice of the Learning Organization* (New York: Doubleday, 1990), p. 354.
5. S. Hawking, *A Brief History of Time: A Reader's Companion* (New York: Bantam, 1992), p. viii.
6. A. Roddick, "Corporate Responsibility," 197.
7. T. Moore, *Care of the Soul: A Guide for Cultivating Depth and Sacredness in Everyday Life* (New York: HarperCollins, 1992), p. 205.
8. B. Moyers, *Healing and the Mind,* 1993 (audiocassette).
9. J. A. Byrne, "He's Gutsy, Brilliant and Carries an Ax," *Business Week,* May 9, 1994, p. 62.

Chapter Six

1. A. Clausi, "U.S. Food System Needs for the 21st Century," *Vital Speeches of the Day,* 1994, *60*(17): 542.
2. J. Paul, "The Oil and Gas Industry," *Vital Speeches of the Day,* 1993, *59*(9): 279.
3. T. Wirth, "Global Conditions," National Press Club speech presented in Washington, D.C., July 12, 1994.
4. Ibid.

5. J. Farinelli, "Succeeding in Business," *Vital Speeches of the Day,* 1994, *60*(17): 531.
6. Ibid.
7. Ibid, p. 533.

Chapter Seven

1. J. Baldwin, *Notes of a Native Son* (Boston: Beacon Press, 1992), p. 7.
2. D. Goldin, "The Light of a New Age," *Vital Speeches of the Day,* 1992, *58*(24): 741.
3. M. Cuomo, *More than Words,* p. 23.
4. T. Wirth, "Global Conditions," July 12, 1994.
5. R. Mahoney, "Politics, Technology and Economic Growth," *Vital Speeches of the Day,* 1993, *59*(20): 627.
6. Ibid.
7. C. King, *The Words of Martin Luther King, Jr.* (New York: Newmarket Press, 1987), p. 83.
8. W. Blake, "Auguries of Innocence," l. 1.

Chapter Eight

1. M. Cuomo, *More than Words,* p. 51.
2. A. Roddick, "Corporate Responsibility," 199.
3. J. Farinelli, "Succeeding in Business," 533.
4. O. Wilde, *The Wit and Wisdom of Oscar Wilde* (New York: Dover, 1959).
5. M. Cuomo, *More than Words,* p. 51.
6. A. Roddick, "Corporate Responsibility," 198.
7. R. W. Terry, *Authentic Leadership: Courage in Action* (San Francisco: Jossey-Bass, 1993), p. 13.
8. A. Roddick, "Corporate Responsibility," 199.

RECOMMENDED READINGS

Bennis, Warren and Nanus, Burt, *Leaders: The Strategies for Taking Charge: The Four Keys of Effective Leadership.* New York: Harper & Row, 1985.

Bennis, Warren, *On Becoming a Leader.* New York: Addison-Wesley, 1992.

Cuomo, Mario, *More Than Words: The Speeches of Mario Cuomo.* New York: St. Martin's Press, 1993.

DePree, Max, *Leadership Jazz.* New York: Doubleday, 1992.

Gergen, Kenneth, *The Saturated Self: Dilemmas of Identity in Contemporary Life.* Basic Books, 1991.

Handy, Charles, *The Age of Unreason.* Cambridge, Mass.: HBS Press, 1990.

Hawking, Stephen, *A Brief History of Time: A Reader's Companion,* New York: Bantam Books, 1992.

Hillman, James and Ventura, Michael, *We've Had a Hundred Years of Psychotherapy and the World's Getting Worse.* San Francisco: Harper, 1992.

King, Corretta, *The Words of Martin Luther King, Jr.* New York: Newmarket Press, 1987.

Kouzes, James M. and Posner, Barry Z., *Credibility: How Leaders Gain and Lose It, Why People Demand It.* San Francisco: Jossey-Bass, 1993.

Kouzes, James M. and Posner, Barry Z., *The Leadership Challenge: How to Get Extraordinary Things Done in Organizations.* San Francisco: Jossey-Bass, 1987.

Leonard, George, *Mastery.* New York: Dutton, 1991.

Melohn, Tom, *The New Partnership,* Essex Junction, Vt.: Oliver Wight Publications, Inc., 1994.

Moore, Thomas, *Care of the Soul: A Guide for Cultivating Depth and Sacredness in Everyday Life.* New York: Harper-Collins, 1992.

Ray, Michael and Rinzler, Alan (eds.). *The New Paradigm in Business.* New York: The Putnam Publishing Groups, 1993.

Senge, Peter, *The Fifth Discipline: The Art and Practice of the Learning Organization.* New York: Doubleday, 1990.

Terry, Robert W., *Authentic Leadership: Courage in Action.* San Francisco: Jossey-Bass, 1993.

Wheatley, Margaret, *Leadership and the New Science.* San Francisco: Berrett-Koehler Publishers, Inc., 1992.

Whyte, David, *The Heart Aroused: Poetry and the Preservation of the Soul in Corporate America.* New York: Doubleday, 1994.

INDEX